Wild Wandering
(21st Adventures with God

Karen Lowe

Shedhead Productions

Antioch Centre
Copperworks Road
Llanelli
SA15 2NE

ISBN: 0-9546989-2-4

First published March 2006 by

Shedhead Productions
Antioch Centre
Copperworks Road
Llanelli
SA15 2NE

Printed in Great Britain by:
Gwasg Gomer
Llandysul
Ceredigion
SA44 4JL

CONTENTS

SITE MAP

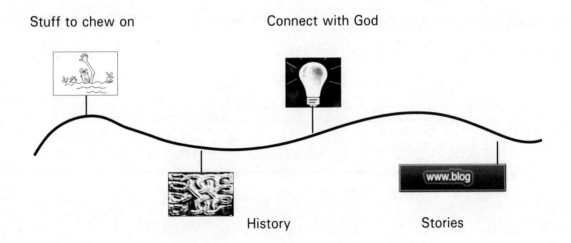

Stuff to chew on

Connect with God

History

Stories

Text, pictures and poetry running through.

DEDICATION

To my amazing husband and children,
Mark, Samuel, Bethany, Rhosanna and Josh -
you inspire me, challenge me, make me laugh and cry.
He knows the cost.
Words can't say how loved you are.

ACKNOWLEDGEMENTS

So many friends are part of this book - it has been an adventure in community even in the writing. Deb you made this book possible it really is a joint effort, a lived out journey, thank you for your friendship. Some of you contributed to the book in more than one way, you may only be thanked once but you are stars!

Book Design	Deb Chapman.
Illustrations and Photographs	Sian Chapron, Paul Mayhill, Karen Lowe, Rhosanna Lowe, Joshua Lowe, Deb Chapman.
Go Deeper and Other Text	Hywel Edwards, Pippa Gardner, Jen Hallet, Steve Lowton, David Pott.
Blogs and Interviews	Steve Porter, Paul Knowlson, Chris Stone, Lucy Keys, Nigel Haddock,Bethany Lowe, Alan Andrews, Rachel Andrews, Tim O'Hare, Ann O'Hare, Phil Smith, Sarah Arnott, Justin Abraham, Dave Vaughan, Sue Erasmus, Sarah Paine,Stuart Watkins, Elizabeth Watkins.
Connect	Zoe Britnell, Ian Mayhew, Beth Landon.
Poetry	Steve Smith.

To all those who critiqued, gave feedback and proof read -
Issie Smith, Steve Hallet, Anna Pienaar, Tom Pienaar,
and Menna Williams (Welsh).

And to everyone who has been a part of mad, wild wandering adventures over the last few years - what a journey!

COMMENDATIONS

"Wild Wandering" is not to be read in one sitting! The testimonies and stories are too rich for such junk digestion! Rather this is a book to be savoured page by page; to be meditated on and chewed over in the company of others and in the company of angels. Hugely challenging, if it fails to take you further to the edge in your walk with Jesus then you have missed the point. A must for those who are seeking to track the wild fire that is beginning to rise from Wales.

Steve Lowton.

"Wild Wandering - Understanding God's purpose that was revealed through our Celtic ancestors and showing us how this can be applied to our lives today. If you want to go deeper with God to reach further and higher, read and apply. Karen doesn't just write about these principles she lives them. "stand at the crossroads and look and ask for the ancient paths". (Jer 6:16.)

Gareth Jones, UK Director, World Horizons and Helen Jones, G.P., Llanelli

"Challenging, thought-provoking, informative and life-changing - Karen Lowe creatively provokes her readers to intimacy with Jesus which will be life-changing. Inspired by our Celtic heritage, she challenges us to wander, led by the Holy Spirit, to seek out the lost, poor, disenfranchised, the very people Jesus spent His time with. Karen is not just a theorist, she continues to walk this out in her own life".

Rob and Cath Whillier, Leaders, The Community Church, Isle of Wight.

INTRODUCTION

INTRODUCTION

"Safety first" is often the way we live our lives, it was not the way that Jesus lived His - it need not be ours! It is time for wild journeys that stretch our safe lives, as the Holy Spirit leads and we take risks. The kindness of Jesus is calling for compassion and miracles in the midst of end-time disaster and pain. Adventurers can discover the passionate heart of the Father and meet with Him in Heavenly Places, there are new dimensions to explore, as He disrupts the predictable and energises the routine.

> What is Wild?
>
> WILD - not domesticated, tame, or cultivated; not civilised; desolate, bleak; very enthusiastic, uncontrolled, unrestrained, unreasonable, untameable by human will, dynamic, exciting, beyond human control.
> (Random dictionary definitions).

All this in a post-modern culture, hungry for experience and connection, hungry for anything spiritual; a pseudo-spirituality won't do it, nice, irrelevant, sanitized Christianity won't do it - we need His help!

Is it wrong to want wild sending, wild serving, lived in the extravagance of his love? Is it wrong to establish the outrageously forgotten truth that he is good and that he cares? I hope not.

Wild is something we can be frightened of, but the Holy Spirit is described as wind and fire. "The wind blows where it pleases" (John 3:8). The early church and the early Salvation Army were baptised in fire - that's wild! In their words -

"By what power is this victory going to be achieved? By fire! The Holy Ghost. Fire is the most potent force in nature. Electricity, light, heat - all are fire. Everything must give way before fire".[1]

There is something of a right wildness that is being released in these days. Jesus as a true friend wants to wake us up and take us on some adventures, he wants "to free the wild possibilities within" us.[2]

Four years ago I was able to spend two months crashed out in a 70's - decor caravan (which in grander moments I thought of as a monastic cell!). He met me in a gentle and painful outpouring of His love. The future wasn't touched on. The effort of surviving the day became the joy of living the day.

He spoke a few words, simple, yet hard to understand - " Walk the land and Carry My Presence". This phrase shaped a journey that is still unfolding.

It became a call to adventure, a call to friendship with the Holy Spirit, a call to hidden peoples and places. It allowed for wild wandering and following Jesus to a throwaway and broken generation. It made the most desperate, the most destroyed, forgotten people and places the priority. The Bible is a book of journeys within an overarching journey and this can be reflected in our lives.

We matter: we can embrace the incredible statement of a second century Christian leader, Irenaeus, " The glory of God is man fully alive, and the life of man is the vision of God". You have the Father's full attention, full focus- His eyes are full of his children, are full of you and full of those who haven't yet met him. He wants us to be fully alive that others may live. The brave, small decisions of our lives, the unglamorous ones, the 'out there' ones count.

In this book "Wild Wandering" there is opportunity to find the safe meeting place of the heart, to encounter desert places and to journey amongst broken communities in this nation and the nations. It has been designed to be interactive, to be written on and to be lived. It attempts to flow out of a place of rest (a seemingly impossible challenge in our Western lives) yet there is an 'unforced rhythm of grace' awaiting our company!

It draws from the Christian Celtic tradition, not as a nice, safely packaged commodity but as a challenge to a rawness of adventure and rest, connection and creativity in the twenty-first century. The historical content is, unashamedly, largely from Wales. This heritage is found in place names and poetry, less so in monuments, than the other Celtic nations, but shapes us still. It tells a hidden story as a magnifying glass to different possibilities.

The book itself is a mosaic of writers, community in different textures and colours. Lived in the day to day in Wales, it has been a wild wander in the writing - Pembrokeshire, Cornwall, Ireland and most profoundly the stones and luminous sea wilderness of the Aran Islands. Inish Mor is the island Brendan visited with his friends to pray and to consult with Enda, a pioneer of the monastic movement in Ireland, before setting off on their

Travel

Barely knew Him,
Hardly dared to call His name.
When He asked me to travel with Him,
I said, "I'd walk on broken glass to be with You".
And meant it.
He asked me to work with Him
I said, "I'd pay to work with You" -
and did.
Set off with wrecked heart,
blue rucksack, no way back
to a different future,
no skills, no fishing
to go back to.
Just desperate
to be with the One who loved me
Out of a hell of a lot of lostness
Just desperate for
others still in a hell of a lot of lostness
still desperate now, still travelling

3

own, extreme, wild wander.

Right now our journey begins as we "go outside, where Jesus is, where the action is - not trying to be privileged insiders, but taking our share in the abuse of Jesus. This insider world is not our home".[3] Let's go outside, seek out the lost and the broken, the desperate and the abused in an extreme wild wander of the type Jesus pioneered. But first we need a detox.

DETOX→INTOXICATED LIFE

DETOX→INTOXICATED LIFE

OVERVIEW

A storm, force 9/10, on Inishmaan fused sky and sea the same in a grey green fury of air too wet to breathe. Cliffs became the beach, rocks the size of houses groaned and moved in the reforming of landscape. The sheer fury of the storm, in its energy and sculpturing of landscape, shut down wind turbines - the power of the wind beyond the delicacy of the blades. The storm with its treacherous currents, a small ferry and a pier that hid freak waves stranded us for two days; disordered our ordered arrangements.

In the huge global reshaping we are living through the Holy Spirit is looking to build in us a delicacy and flexibility of strength which will flow with the power He is releasing worldwide. Safety is no longer to be found in the structures and in the ways life has always been. Safety is found in a fresh yielding and a fresh following of Him. But how can we detox from a culture that consumes?

Detox happens as we gain a fresh revelation of the Kingdom and its challenge to a dominant culture in church and society. It happens as the last in our world, the poor and the rejected are valued as the first. The kingdom is a revolution of the seemingly insignificant, a party celebrating an upside down world turned the right way - a party for the "poor, the maimed, the lame and the blind" (Luke 14:13).

The place to detox from the dominant culture of the day is in the desert. John the Baptist knew all about this. Detox for John was about freedom from the pursuit of power and the norms and games of empire, religious and otherwise. He was positioned in the desert to hear the word from God about the defining moment in history. He recognised the Messiah when He came, received Him and led others to do the same. In obedience He baptised the One above whom the heavens opened and delighted to decrease as Jesus increased.

Johns' message was one of Extreme Surrender, Extreme Obedience, Extreme Sacrifice, Extreme Devotion. It was a call to repentance - a call to turn and allow a deep exposing of masks, shadow selves and desert souls.

DESERT DETOX

For us it could be confronting self-obsession in a space - a place of silence and solitude. Allowing the compulsive drive for definition and esteem; the frenzy of being materially

CONNECT - TAKE TIME OUT IN A QUIET PLACE TO DO AN 'EXAMEN'.

An 'Examen' is an old religious term for looking seriously at your life through the kind, impossible-to-fool eyes of Jesus. It may involve focusing on particular issues. It may cover general or specific time frames.

A Practical Desert Detox - Examine

- What happens when you spend an hour on your own in silence?

- What happens when you record all your spending for a week - are you materially possessed?

- Choose to do unseen acts of service and kindness over a month - how has that impacted desires for recognition and applause?

- Read a newspaper, watch the news, examine your reactions and ask the Holy Spirit for His perspective.

- Do a "Thomas a Kempis" at the beginning of the day -
" In the morning form your intention, and at night examine your conduct, what you have done, said, and thought during the day, for in each of these you may have often offended both God and your neighbour." [1] Ouch!

possessed - to be overwhelmed by the receiving of an unreasonable love. The cult of title, publicity and the moment of fame; the worship and compulsion of now leading to empty nowhere - displaced by a taste of eternity. The jarring fragments of disconnected and scattered life drowning in noise - eased into sleep on the Fathers chest. A major salt scrub treatment, light-therapy exposure transforming us into salt and light subversives.

Are we living beyond what the culture says is final, accepting boundaries the Father hasn't called us to accept? In the flowering of Celtic Christianity

"No subversive ever dares anything big. He is always carrying secret messages, planting suspicion that there is something beyond what the culture says is final."
Eugene H. Peterson [2]

HISTORY

Christianity had reached Wales by the second century and by the third we had our first recorded martyrs - Aaron and Julius in Caerleon, Gwent. In the era after the Emperor Constantine declared himself a Christian, it is likely that Christianity flourished in the areas where there was a stronger Roman influence. In the fifth century when the Romans left Britain pagan tribes attacked churches and killed Christians.

However, in Wales Christianity flourished in what became known as the "Age of the Saints". The roots of this awakening were linked to the missionary work of Martin of Tours. Many influenced by him became the original apostles in the land, what some would describe as the 'aboriginal' apostles. There was Dyfrig of south west Wales and Caldey, Illtyd of the incredible community and training school at Llantwit Major; Deiniol whose main sphere of influence was in Gwynedd moving out from Bangor, Beuno was also associated with Gwynedd, from Clynnog Fawr he influenced much of north Wales, and of course there was David! The Age of the Saints left it's mark on the very fabric of the land, not least in place names. (The "wild wanderings" of the Celtic saints meant that the message of Jesus was taken all over Wales and into Europe and beyond - these are some of the wild wanderers whose stories we will be looking at alongside those from other Celtic nations.) The place names speak of a nation coloured once a house of prayer and names beginning with "Llan" or "Tre" speak of an enclosure around a place of prayer linked to a saints name. "Dysserth" speaks of deserts, "Mynach" and "Mynachlog" of monasteries, "Abaty" of Abbey, and "Bettws" of house of prayer/chapel of ease. There is also the much later naming of villages after the chapels, giving a biblical feel to many areas in the land, this usage flowing naturally from a deep well of spirituality and from walking the land back and forth to the meeting places. The chapel names reflected something of the values of the founders.

there was a fresh explosion of creativity, the arts. There was an expectation that the supernatural world of the gospels was for real. Varied expressions of community were established and nations were impacted. There was an embracing of much that had been lost from the days of the early Church. They were incarnating Jesus in a post Christian, pagan culture - so are we! There are many differences, obvious and not so, but much too learn.

We carry the stories of heaven's truths luminous with humanity and hope but dare we engage? In drawing close to Jesus it must be possible to connect in new ways with contemporary culture. Cynicism can be confronted with wonder, boredom with awe. If contemplation involves gazing on the glory in the face of Jesus, the wisdom and beauty there must surely touch the physical world, which draws its life from Him.

How do we draw close? One way to draw close is through 'soaking', a contemporary take on contemplative prayer, silence and solitude. Soaking prayer, amongst other things, allows the Father to heal us and can take us on a journey into the meeting place of the heart.

The meeting place of the heart also becomes the doorway to literally explore the 'heavenly

CONNECT - WITH THE GLORY - SOAK

Soaking prayer is resting in the presence of Jesus.

- Lie down somewhere comfortable.
- Put a worship c.d. on or if that is too distracting lie quietly.
- Yield afresh to Jesus.
- Ask the Father to set the limits and boundaries on the time.
- Welcome the Holy Spirit to come.
- If there is a lot of inner noise give it all to Jesus , the worries, distractions etc, then keep focusing back on Jesus, welcome the Holy Spirit again.
- Keep going - the more you do this the easier it becomes to find connection.
- Afterwards maybe journal what He says to you, or what you see, learn, experience.

"During the time here at Daybreak I have been led to an inner place where I have not been before. It is the place within me where God has chosen to dwell. It is the place where I am held safe in the embrace of an all loving Father who calls my name and says 'You are My beloved son, on you My favour rests.' 'It is the place where I can taste of the joy and peace that are not of this world,' Jesus says, 'anyone who loves Me will keep My word and My Father will love him and We shall come and make Our home in him" Henri Nouwen [3]

places' of Ephesians 1:20. Jesus has torn the veil, ripped open the heavens, He is the ladder, He is the door, He has made it possible for us to have access to the heavens, to come before the throne. In the words spoken to John (Revelation 4: 1) when he saw a door standing open in heaven we can "come up."

Jesus has made this a now reality, maybe it is only our fears or insecurities that stop us. How much do we really believe that Gods power to bless us, to keep us, and to lead us is greater than the enemy's power to deceive. In Jesus we can literally be an open heaven and access an open heaven wherever we go. Jesus has pioneered the way at total cost to himself, He is calling us to adventure with Him into heavenly places - will we?

What does it mean to walk this out in the everyday? What does it mean to walk the land and carry His presence, to be an open heaven and access an open heaven wherever we go? How can this be one expression of a de-toxed, intoxicated life?

It is simple. It is not prayer walking, excellent as that is, although you do pray and you do walk. It is about seeking out the people the Holy Spirit has lined up for you to meet. It involves talking to people, listening to people and praying for the sick. It involves being bold enough to initiate a conversation, get involved in an act of kindness or give a gift of food.

"We decided as a group of young people to do this stuff. We ended up meeting someone who had been prayed for in our youth club a few months before because he had a bone disease, he couldn't do sport and things like that. He said that after the prayer he had got a lot better. It was great to pray for him again for more, he seemed really happy. We ended up praying for a policeman, for someone who was an alcoholic and drunk - he cried, and for people on drugs. Some people tried to walk faster to get away! There were quite a few people around for a Sunday morning".   Bethany Lowe

It is spontaneous. It is doing the stuff that Jesus did. It is not a programme or a new evangelistic method- it is about seeking His face so His face can be seen in simple, ordinary, extraordinary, day-to-day ways. Programme is replaced with encounter and joins in the mystery of the Creator hidden in a few pounds of baby flesh. We need to 'be there'. Woody Allen's "80% of life is just showing up" - seems appropriate!

It is also doing the stuff the Celtic Christians had done in a nation which had heard something of the message of Jesus but lost it. Deitrich Bonhoeffer called for "a new kind of

"The territories that the Irish monks sought were the unknown and uninhabited lands beyond the horizon, the special places, the wondrous lands to be revealed by God. In the apt phrase of the time they were the Promised Lands. To reach these farthest territories was a heavenly gift: to be able to live in them, isolated from the evils of the world was an even greater prize. There can seldom have been a stronger drive to probe the unknown in the entire history of human exploration. It was the quintessential motive for exploration at almost any price, and there is no reason why it should not have brought them across the Atlantic."[4] Tim Severin

CONNECT - LIFE MAP

Explore, connect with your life journey so far....

Draw a picture of your life's journey - A Life Map - an image that conveys your journey so far. It may be a river, a game of snakes and ladders, a mountain - anything you like - e.g. river - *mark on it the points, events, circumstances, the times which have been significant for you - answer two questions for each -

What?

Why?

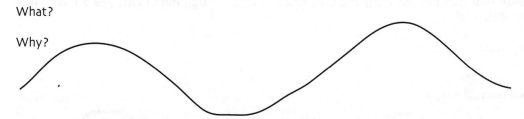

- If you are very old (!), have lived a colourful life, or a detail person, etc (!) you may want to take a segment, or a few years of your life.

- When you have done this ask Jesus what He sees as the significant events, circumstances, times etc and why?

- Are they the same or different?

- What does this tell you? Ask Him to help you in reflecting (thinking back deeply) on this.

monasticism - a life of uncompromising adherence to the Sermon on the Mount".

The language of a new monasticism may seem hard to relate to, the message of the sermon on the mount even more so.

To simply walk the land and be the hands, eyes, voice, heart and power of Jesus to someone in need is both scary and exciting. There are no pre-requisites, no forms to fill in, no 'red-tape' to comply with, and no conditions to satisfy.

Wild wandering has a taste of the journey Jesus made from Heaven - a deliberate journey for the sake of the lost. It is the deliberate choice to seek out the discarded, unvalued people in any community - often the hidden, or not so hidden poor. It can be a voyage of displaced compassion - connecting with those we do not understand, or who do not understand us.

LIFE MAP - Two Years

Just my reflections and what I feel Jesus was showing me about my experiences in the two years before moving away to university. By mapping out significant times and dates, situations, prophetic words received, etc. I was able to trace God's hand. Now He has shown me how, and to some extent why He has brought to where I am now. I realise that God has done significantly more in and through me in two years than I was ever aware of...

Lucy Keys

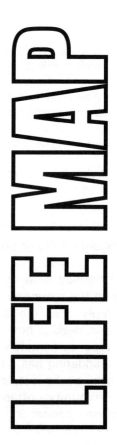

Two Years…

Two short years - significant?
Has two years shaped a life?
Risks taken, Character shaken -
Yet built
Running to and running from
Brokenness with Restoration - Painfully loved
Building childlike maturity, confidence, humility
Words spoken:
Home, Cymru, The Nations…then hope forsaken
Destiny without purpose - sometimes
Like running without limbs
Being fully equipped yet utterly dependant.
Betrayed then Reconciled - Testing Times.
Envisioned and Strengthened - His Fire Burning
Deep Roots - Green Shoots
Friends - Now Family
His Faithfulness and Fathering
Moulded in His Hands
Home, where my heart is …
… Two Years

Lucy Keys

HISTORY - TIMELINE CELTIC CHRISTIANITY

BC   The Celts, emerge as distinctive tribal people groups, but retreat to the fringes of Europe as the Roman Empire advances.

AD 40/50 - The Celts of Galatia come to faith through Paul. Legend tells of the arrival of Christianity in Britain early in the first century - possibly through travellers trading tin in Cornwall- legend cites Joseph of Arimathea as one of those early traders.

43 - 410 - Roman occupation of Southern Britain Christianity is introduced.

200 -   By at least this time Christianity has reached Wales as Aaron and Julius were martyred in Caerleon Gwent.

313 -   Emperor Constantine makes Christianity the official religion this leads to major decline into immorality and respectability - leading to a counter culture movement in the desert - the Desert Fathers.

390 -   Martin of Tours in Gaul and his disciple Ninian in Whithorn, Scotland, inspired by the Desert Fathers, set up radical monastic communities.

410 -   Romans leave Britain and Anglo Saxons invade and destroy churches, except those in the Celtic margins.

435 -   Ireland develops as a light for the nations as over the next 100years Patrick, Brendan and many others see it become a "land of saints".

450 -   Wales and Cornwall become the same as mission communities are planted by Illtyd David, Samson - they were also inspired by Martin of Tours and the desert fathers .

563 -   Columba brings the gospel to Sotland.

591 -   Columbanus and other wandering monks establish mission communities all over Europe

597 -   The Pope sends Augustine to England.

635 -   Aidan is sent from Iona to Lindisfarne and with Hilda at Whitby sends missionaries to the Midlands, South and East.

664 -   TheSynod of Whitby - The Celtic church begins to yield ground to the Rome church.

690 -   The Book of Kells epitomises a flourishing of learning and the arts centred around monastic communities.

793 - Monastic communities destroyed in a century of Viking Invasions.

There are adventures
of wild wandering to
be had in these and
in many more landscapes,
explored and unexplored,
in the supernatural realm
as well as on the earth.

It is not too late...

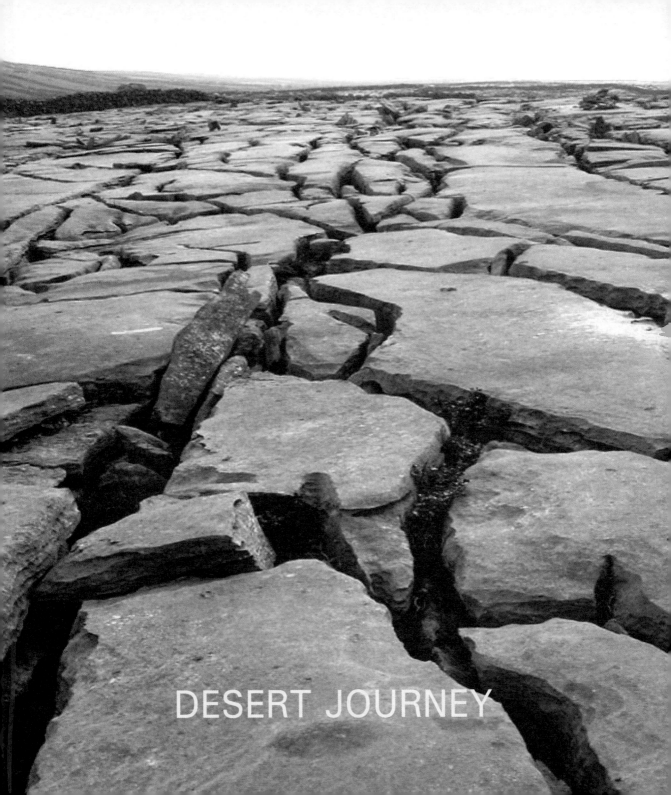

DESERT JOURNEY

DESERT JOURNEY

For John the Baptist the desert became the stage to welcome the greatest moment in history, the margins became the highway. For the Desert Fathers, the men and women who made the deserts their home in the 3rd and 4th centuries, their lives were a protest vote against the death by respectability that Constantine had brought to the Church. "Monasticism was a protest...the hermit fled not so much from the world as from the world in the church".[1] They were people who made their home on the edges of society; their lives spoke of passionate devotion, a battle in the secret place to see the kingdom come. They saw their solitude as more than a self-serving quest for spiritual enlightenment but as a gift of willingness to fight for breakthrough against the demonic forces that were confronting both church and society.

Desert is physical place, it is also a counter-culture way of life and prayer is its counter-culture craziness. It is a culture where productivity and usefulness is measured in different waits and colours. It is a place of the burning passion of an unreasonable love and an unreasonable desire for God. It is a place to become truly alive. Heavens truths are explored

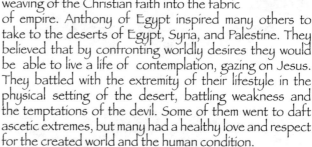

HISTORICAL BACKGROUND

In Egypt in the 3rd and 4th century there was a major reaction to the corruption of Christianity through Constantine and his weaving of the Christian faith into the fabric of empire. Anthony of Egypt inspired many others to take to the deserts of Egypt, Syria, and Palestine. They believed that by confronting worldly desires they would be able to live a life of contemplation, gazing on Jesus. They battled with the extremity of their lifestyle in the physical setting of the desert, battling weakness and the temptations of the devil. Some of them went to daft ascetic extremes, but many had a healthy love and respect for the created world and the human condition.

The Desert Fathers and Mothers influenced the Celtic church of Britain and Ireland. In Wales 'dysserth' - Welsh for desert - is a common place name as is 'disart' in Ireland.

There was even a wannabe St Anthony in Llanstephan (monks often took their name from a spiritual hero who had influenced them). In the story-telling Celtic crosses of the day there is one in Nash with a carving of St. Anthony and St. Paul of Thebes. There is also one in Penmon which shows Anthony battling against demonic beasts.

Empire - a large group of countries or people under one authority. Something resembling a political empire especially an extensive territory or enterprise under single domination or control.
(The New Penguin English Dictionary).

and tested in earth's furnace, the stark light of heaven sharpened on earth's bones.

The barrenness of landscape reflects a place of emptying and at times the inner landscape is one of barrenness and desolation. It is a place of yielding where less full of ourselves we can become filled with Him.

"It may become impossible to believe that this road goes anywhere at all except to a desolation full of dry bones - the ruin of all our hopes and good intentions".[3] It seems that the place of dying can in the end become a place of resurrection and new beginnings. It is certainly a place of training and a place where we allow the Father to strip away the unhelpful, unnecessary elements in our life that lead us away from Him. From this palace of emptying it seems easier to identify with the poor and marginalised. This is not just a one-off encounter but a lifelong rhythm of withdrawal and engagement.

The word desert literally means, abandonment, the word hermit derives from it. In Leviticus, it is the cursed place, the lifeless place of death because there is no water. In the Bible desert has many faces as the stories of desert, garden and city intertwine. It is the place where Jacob battled and met with God. It is a place of naming and encounters, of revelation, beginnings and commissioning.

17

CONNECT - DESERT TRAINING

Get familiar with the spiritual disciplines that help in shaping up and working out. The spiritual disciplines are, "a means of receiving God's grace….(They) allow us to place ourselves before God so He can transform us" [4]

Biblical Meditation - chew on a passage of scripture. If it helps the chewing ask what does it mean and what should I do? Joshua 1:8

Contemplation/ Listening Prayer/Soaking - are slightly different doors through which to gaze on Jesus.

• Contemplation emphasises a focused inner seeing and experiencing of Him in silence.

• Listening prayer - listening to what He wants to say, asking Him questions and listening for the answers in quietness - "His still small voice."

• Soaking - marinating, basking, revelling, resting in His presence.

Secrecy - starve the need for attention or applause - Matt 6: 1-8

Fasting - freeing us to feast on Jesus - Isaiah 58:1-11.

Study - providing a framework for relationship not pride - John 8:31.

Solitude - choosing God's company and your own.

Silence - shutting up on the inside and on the outside in order to hear Him - Psalm 46:10.

Reflection - looking back to learn in His presence - Psalm 65: 1-13.

Service - looking out for others for His sake - John 13:14-15.

Community - lived out relationships with Jesus central - 1 Cor 12: 12-19.

Simplicity - a lifestyle and attitude of restraint - Matt 6:19-21- balanced of course by generosity to others.

Confession - accountability in humility - James 5:16.

Choose a discipline, ENCOUNTER Him in it, walk out the DISCIPLINE of it, enjoy the FRUITFULNESS of it ....choose a discipline.

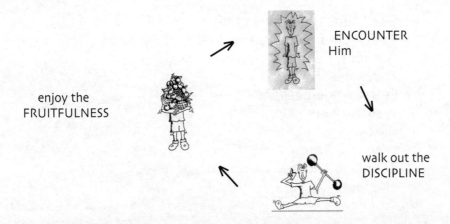

ENCOUNTER
Him

enjoy the
FRUITFULNESS

walk out the
DISCIPLINE

This pattern of encounter, discipline and then fruitfulness provides good conditions for change to occur, it is a way of sowing to the Spirit, as through His grace He works in our lives.

Ian Mayhew

Jesus went to meet with His Father in the mountains of Judea, getting away from the crowds to pray, maybe in a cave or in the sunlight. Paul followed his encounter and commissioning by God with "desert time"; "But when God, who set me apart from birth and called me by His grace, was pleasedto reveal His Son in me so that I might preach Him among the gentiles, I did not consult any man, nor did I go up to Jerusalem to see those who were apostles before I was, but I immediately went into Arabia and later returned to Damascus". Galatians 1:15-17.

The desert was probably where Paul reflected on his upturned life. The desert silence became "a bed for revelation to rest on" [7] where he received heavenly visions . The desert of testing became a garden of intimacy - a paradise. It became an oasis.

Paul was following the pattern of commissioning lived out by Jesus - baptism in water and with the Holy Spirit, the voicing of the Father's approval and love under an open heaven, followed by the temptations in the wilderness, before the release to ministry.

In the desert Jesus faced and passed the tests the Israelites failed in their desert

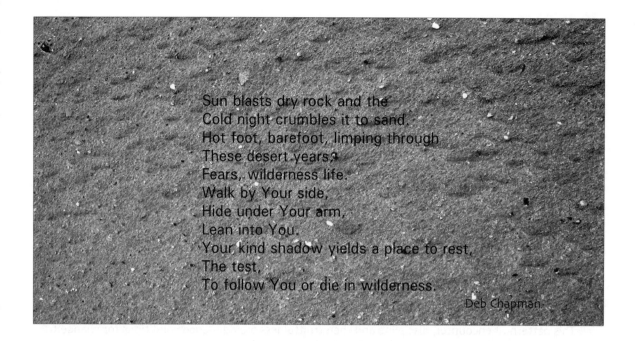

Sun blasts dry rock and the
Cold night crumbles it to sand.
Hot foot, barefoot, limping through
These desert years?
Fears, wilderness life.
Walk by Your side,
Hide under Your arm,
Lean into You.
Your kind shadow yields a place to rest,
The test,
To follow You or die in wilderness.

Deb Chapman.

wanderings; issues of materialism, authority, true worship; issues faced with a yielded heart and truth words - 'Desert time' revealing true authority, true sonship.

The desire to belong and to connect with others is a fundamental part of our humanity, as is the desire to belong and connect to land. Today it seems hard to engage with land in a way that is not superficial - yet superficial or not the desire is still there.

In Psalm 103:15,16 one of the marks of death is that we are no longer remembered by our 'place'-

"As for a man, his days are like grass,
He flourishes like a flower of the field
The wind blows over it and it is gone,
And its place remembers it no more".

Jesus measures the cost of discipleship in the loss of land as well as in the loss of family. "And everyone who has left houses or brothers or sisters or father or mother or children or fields for My sake will receive a hundred times as much and will inherit eternal life" (Matthew 19:29).

DESERT BLOG

The monks lived on the margins of society and the church. Their lives and words challenged both. The Sayings of the Desert Fathers are the mini-blogs of 127 abbas (fathers) and 3 ammas (mothers) in 1202 sayings. They were sayings born in the desert, drawn out by hungry visitors, passed on by word of mouth and eventually written down.

"Anthony was to compare a monk out of the desert to a fish out of water. And when a philosopher asked him how he could endure without books his long solitude, he would point to the mountainous wilderness around him: 'My book, O philosopher, is the nature of the created things, and it is present when I will, for me to read the words of God." [5]

Amma Syncletica said: "There are many who live in the mountains and behave as if they were in the town; they are wasting their time. It is possible to be a solitary in one's mind whilst living in a crowd; and it is possible for those who are solitaries to live in the crowd of their own thoughts." [6]

Abba Poemen: "Passions work in four stages - first in the heart; secondly, on the face; thirdly, in words; and fourthly, it is always essential not to render evil for evil in deeds. If you can purify your heart, passion will not reveal itself in your expression; but if it reaches your face then take care not to speak; and if you do speak, at least cut the conversation short in case you do render evil for evil.'

Abba Poemen: "Is it better to speak or to be silent?" The old man said to him: "The person who speaks for God's sake does well; the person who keeps silent for God's sake also does well" [6]

Abba Poemen: Sin is to be avoided, the sinner is to be embraced. "Why hate the person who has harmed you? It is not the person who has done the wrong. Hate the sickness, but do not hate the sick person."

Abba Lot went to see Abba Joseph and said to him, "Abba, as far as I can I say my little office [prayers], I fast a little, I pray and meditate, I live in peace and as far as I can I purify my thoughts. What else can I do?' Then the old man stood up and stretched his hands towards heaven. His fingers became like ten lamps of fire and he said to him, "If you will, you can become all flame". [6]

"The time of business does not with me differ from the time of prayer, and in the noise and clatter of my kitchen, while several persons are at the same time calling for different things, I possess God in as great tranquillity as if I were upon my knees at the blessed sacrament." [8]
Brother Lawrence 1611-1691

Post it Notes - questions for reflection, connection in a full-on day!
Post it Notes to stick on busy minds

- Do a 'Brother Lawrence 'practice the presence of Jesus' while washing up, cooking or cleaning. Search your life for a God moment - Did I bring Jesus into my world in some way today?
- Ask the Holy Spirit to speak to you through some aspect of your surroundings today.
- Reflect on how He might want to release wonder, awe and play into your life today.
- Ask Him to show you a situation, people or person He wants you to serve in some way.
- Really listen to someone.
- Learn a verse from the Bible and chew on it, think about it throughout the day.
- How does Jesus want to demonstrate through you that His kingdom is not simply words but power?
- In what way can you encourage gratitude and thankfulness to bubble up.
- Reflect on an incident in the day. Ask Jesus for His perspective on it and anything He wants to show you through it.

GO DEEPER - FOCUS ON LAND

LAND - THE MEETING PLACE

Land is the meeting place between God and man. The garden was a specific place on earth where, in the cool of the day, the Lord came to meet with Adam and Eve. We are created to enjoy friendship with the Father of Creation. He knows our hearts and He wants to share His. Where you live is a physical place for the 'habitation', the constant dwelling of His Presence!

As you read through the Old Testament, it is significant to see that many were led by the Lord to different places and the first thing they did was to build an altar to the Lord. Altars were places of great importance to Noah, Abraham, Isaac and Jacob. They were built as a place of worship; a place of offering; a place of dedication; and a place of establishing His Name.

1. Abraham built an altar on arriving in Canaan (Gen 12:5, 7), and Bethel (Gen 12:8) and Hebron (Gen 13:18).
2. Noah did the same when he came out of the ark (Gen 8:20).

Land or earth is the physical geography. Land is a meeting place with God and it is only the Body of Christ through worship and intimate communion with God who can bring His presence tangibly on earth today.

Hywel Rhys Edwards

The Desert Fathers had their wilderness but sun and sand were in short supply in the Celtic lands! So sacred place for them was found in caves, on islands, in deep forests, of the kind still found in Ystradfellte, and mountains. Place names like Merthyr Tydfil coming from the Greek Martyrdom - (martur) don't refer to literal martyrs but to those who choose the long martyrdom of a life of solitude in a wilderness place.

Desert walk ... John Scott of Ystradfellte with its 'deep forests' and barren heights decided in 2002 to walk around Wales and pray. Family and parish responsibilities have meant that he can only do it in chunks of a day or two at a time. He walks 15 to 20 miles a day. So far he has ended up swimming across estuaries (Tremadog) cut off on beaches (Red Wharfe, Ynys Mon), stranded in the dark (Monmouth), trying to find footpaths anywhere, negotiating caravan parks everywhere - why? He is simply praying, often without words, that the barren heights, the 'Moel' of Wales will flow again with rivers, that a spiritually barren nation will once again spring life and that where there are green shoots of life emerging they will be sustained and emerge in strength. It sounds a priestly kind of walk to me.

There is a yearning in many people to find the solitary desert places and connect there. For some people it is an enforced solitude as it was for Patrick, slave and shepherd on the Antrim hills of Ireland.

"More and more did my love of God my awe of Him and my faith increase. My spirit was moved so that in a single day I would say as many as a hundred prayers and in the night a like number, even when I was staying in the woods and on the mountains. And I used to rise before dawn for prayer in snow and frost and rain and I used to feel no ill effect and there was no slackness in me. I now realise it was because the Spirit was glowing in me".[9]

Sometimes a desert place can catch us by surprise. I had known about Burry Holms and something of its history but never 'seen' it.

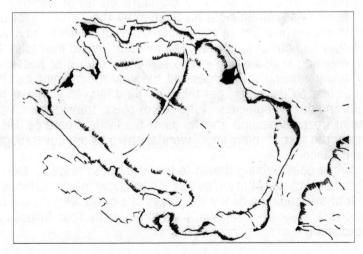

Burry Holm - aerial view

www.blog

DESERT BLOGG

Yesterday, a special day, rested in His presence, walked the land with Him, saw the dark ash, burnt ground - the aftermath of wildfire - but no green shoots and found an Island.

All my life it seems I have wanted an island and for 20 years there has been one under my nose. An island with sea thrift, sheer cliffs, tidal, textured in history of saints, of Cadoc and Cenydd and ring forts. Have seen it many times from the beach and not seen it, sat with my back on the rocks, turned away from the ragged causeway and still not seen it.

Is this like the divine dimension when that which is most obvious and unseen cannot be seen until eyes are opened? ... I want to lay my head on the stones and dream, to see the ladder and the angels, but will it be that sort of gate or another darker one?

Thursday - here now, cut off by the tide, sleeping bag thrown down on a grass mattress on top of the island. Light a fire where the Culdees built their oratory. Slabs of wood burn in cracked - fire- streets, paving stones of leaf green give promise of the new. The night is beautiful and still, gaze at the stars, remember a few shapes and names. Break bread, drink wine and pray over the redemptive gift of the island. Meaning seems to be where the margins meet in rock and sky in the rhythm of the sea's breath. Can this be a place to find You, a place of encounter?

In the night feel hot and sick, dream of battling with demons, the holders of a darkened gate, this island, and win. Now lying drinking tea as the sun pastels the edge of a grey morning, a young gull is magnificent and golden against the grey light, even the butterflies look big in the pared-down life of this island - and still the planes of war fly.

Is anyone alive? There is no one in sight on September the 12th - a year on from 9/11- what happened in the closing hours of 11 remembered? This seems to have an echo of the Desert Fathers. Did they feel anxious, cut off from news of world events in their day?

Still reaching for meaning in this island not to somehow own it or possess it, but walk lightly, connecting, understanding the bridges and the way the margins can became gates to heaven's sight.......rest on the grass, get taken on third heaven journey - heights of His throne, snowy peaks and dazzling glaciers of the sea of glass, translucent crystal peaks and troughs, mountains of frozen seascape, the wings of the living creatures, His voice as the sound of many waters the roar of many seas, wonder sharp as air cut through with winter as worlds collide and dance.

Pillars of fire along the coast, young drawn to the wilderness places... Don't have to be, do everything, only what You ask of me. You ask me to show mercy, listen, simplicity, call the green shoots out of the land. The dark wind plays cat's paws with the white edge where the waters meet the rock spine of the island. I am heavy with Your fullness in this empty space, this holy desolation.

BURRY HOLMS HISTORY AND LEGEND

Burry Holms (Holms is a Norse word for Island) is a tiny tidal island off Llangennith beach the other end from the dramatic Worms Head, it rises 30m above the sea and is no more than 400m long. Yet, it holds in miniature much of the history of Gower, and of Wales itself. It is a place of beginnings, one of the known dwelling places of of the Mesolithic inhabitants of Wales. It also carries a similar history to many of the islands and islets of Wales. Burry Holms was one of a number of these 'dysserth' places which drew the monks in their desire to meet with God in wilderness. This was Cenydd's place where he first came as a hermit before establishing an oratory there in the 6th century. It is not hard to imagine him landing from his coracle with a deep sense of homecoming, particularly if the legends about him have even the slightest grain of truth.

Cenydd was supposed to have been cast adrift as a baby in a wicker basket in the Loughor estuary by parents hoping to conceal their adultery. He survived the ordeal and grew up - fed by gulls - either on Worms Head or Burry Holms !

A church was established in Llangennith itself. It was possibly the same sort of connection that existed between Aberdaron and Bardsey, Penmon and Priestholm, where hermitages and places of retreat were partnered with vibrant communities.

In the 11th century Burry Holms became the site of a Culdees' monastery - under Caradoc of Rhos. The Culdees were a reform movement originating from Ireland who wanted to call the monasteries and the Church back to its original vision. Burry Holms was the only Culdees' monastery that we know of in South Wales and may have been the home of some of the monastic poets whose work found its way into the 'Black books', 'Llyfr Ddu' of Carmarthen and probably the home of some wannabe poets whose poems didn't quite cut it for the day.

View from Burry Holms

Here is a poem from the Llyfr Du Caerfyrddyn, they 'seem to belong to the tradition in Celtic lands of hermit poetry - incandescent pieces created out in the open, in the God-created wild, much like their counterparts in Ireland'.

Gogonedauc argluit hanpich guell.
Aeth uendicco de egluis, a chagell.
A.   kagell. ac egluis.
A.   vastad. a diffuis.
A.   teir finhuan yssit.
Due uch guint. ac vn uch eluit.
A.   yr isgaud ar dit.
A.   siric a perwit.
Ath uendiguis te awraham pen fit.
A.   vuchet tragiuit.
A.   adar a guenen.
A.   attpaur. a dien.
Ath uendigus te aron a moesen.
A.   vascul a femen.
A.   seithnieu a ser.
A.   awir. ac ether.
A.   llevreu a llyther.
A.   piscaud in hydiruer.
A.   kywid. a gueithred.
A.   tyuvod a thydued.
A.   y saul da digoned.
Ath uendigaf de argluit gogoned.
Gogonedauc. a. h. G.

('Hail, glorious Lord! May church and chancel praise You. May chancel and church praise You. May valley floor and mountainside praise You. May the three well-springs, two above the wind and one above the earth, praise You. May night and day praise You. May silk and fruit-tree praise You. Abraham, founder of the faith, praised You. May eternal life praise You. May birds and bees praise You. May after-grass and fresh shoots praise You. Aaron and Moses praised You. May male and female praise You. May the seven days and the stars praise You. May the air and the upper atmosphere praise You. May the books and letters praise You. May fishes in the river praise You. May thought and action praise You. May sand and soil praise You. May all the good that has been done praise You. I praise You, Lord of Glory! Hail, glorious Lord!')[10]

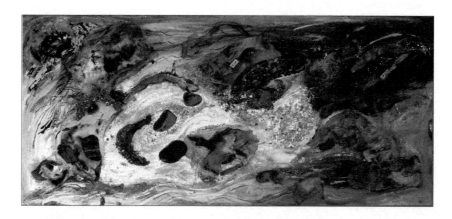

CONNECT

Find a 'desert' place and spend time there outside. Remember much of the gospel narrative took place outside - as did much of the Old Testament.

Ask Jesus to set the framework for the time - the framework might be not to have one!

"A group of us decided to do an outdoor, overnight, silent retreat on cliffs above a Gower beach. We had some gaps where we could talk but there were seemingly unending hours of silence. There were the usual distractions of, mad drunk people (not in the group!), overexcited dogs and over-responsible Gower residents. The most remarkable thing was the differences in what we each experienced, even though we had been in the same place over the same time.

People faced up to sin issues, others had a great time enjoying being outside, some struggled with stopping and the silence. Several worked through profound issues of healing, for others it marked a key transition in their lives, a few received some healing but were frustrated that more didn't happen, someone got translated in the spirit and rather shocked found themself in other nations, others enjoyed it but felt it hadn't been particularly significant for them. Most people would have fitted into more than one of those categories over the time."

Why tell the story? It simply demonstrates that there is no set response and no definitive encounter.

ENCOUNTER HIM IN DESERT

A poem from that time....

Here I am

Here I am
Perched, wedged between the rocks
Skin and bones squeezed between these
hard places
Pushed back, confined by incoming tide.
Hiding from the scorching sun.
And doesn't this describe my life?
Seeking a hiding place from
the unchangeable, unarguable elements
the absolutes of life.
The sea, the rocks and the sand
That's shaped where I've ended up.
My skin and bones are soft
in comparison to these elements.
There are some things you can't argue
Or even dialogue with.
I feel very human this morning
Very aware of vulnerability.
Yes, and now the tide turns.
I see the high tide mark on the cliffs,
The waterline on the rocks.

The tide has turned
And I need to move out with the tide.
God says the tide has turned
In my life
And I can begin to move out
From all my restrictions
And explore again.
The tide has turned
I go down to the freshly emerging sand
And mark my new footprints
And claim this new ground as mine.
As the tide retreats I continue this expansion.
Then I take my shoes off, Holy ground,
Splashing into the waters.
Tears rolling down my cheeks,
God, this is intoxicating.

Then two swimmers swim round
from the next bay and enter my cove.
And the moment was over

Steve Smith

JOURNEY OF THE HEART

JOURNEY OF THE HEART

"A brother came to Scetis to visit Abba Moses and asked him for a word. The old man said to him: 'Go sit in your cell and your cell will teach you everything'".

What is a cell - a prison for naughty monks?! A cell in 'Desert Father' terms is simply a room, a hut, a cave, where you shut the door on intrusion and spend time alone in the light of His presence or absence. It is not about 'personal space' or 'time for me'. Self-discovery and realisations may happen but they are not the focus. The happening is in our response to the One who first loved us. It is the place of a patient wait of love, the place of encounter with Him in radiant fire or in hours of seemingly fruitless greyness. Patience the only clock as culture and eternity collide in our 21st century obsessions.

The cell is like the desert, it is an interior as well as exterior location - except in a cell you can shut the door! It is an exterior meeting place that provides a physical environment of time, solitude and silence for an inner meeting with Jesus.

CELL BLOG

Abba Ammonas: "Go sit in your cell and engrave it on your heart".[1]

Abba Poeman: "We have been taught ... to close the door of our tongues". [2]

Thomas Kelly: "Deep within us all there is an amazing inner sanctuary of the soul, a holy place, a divine centre a speaking voice, to which we may continually return. Our love is not an originating love but a responding love. 1John 4:19 'We love because He first loved us".[2]

Brother Roger of Taize: "In every one lies a solitude that no human intimacy can fill; and there God encounters us".[2]

The decision to shut the door and spend time with God is a gift of trust we give to Him. The embrace of silence and solitude helps us to receive from Him a fresh gift of wonder. It is about the priority of His presence; adventuring in listening. "Staying silent and staying put" are the essence of the cell. Yet to live in solitude simply to escape from difficult relationships is no escape at all - relational pain makes solitude an endless roundabout with no exit except true resolution.

Solitude might, in the first instance, require a physical space in which to 'be alone.' In the end it can be found in the meeting place of the heart, a place of His presence that can be stepped into at will.

First steps may be looking for that physical space!

CONNECT

Identify your own "cell" - weird, less weird and more weird solutions illustrated! - use it on a regular basis.

"For us the desert can be like an oasis - we have so much clutter in our lives normally that we need to find a more simple place to be alone with God." Beth Landon.

Sheds

In search of a hut
A shed in open landscape,
A place to shut one door and open another
Into a layered world of prayer and creativity.
A pile of stones
To lean a head and dream
Until a way is opened.

The monks had beehives
On a fang in the sea's spit,
Dylan had a garage
hung over an estuary.
Both in the outside, inside.

Where is my shed?
I am jealous of the monks and Dylan.
In Llanelli: they say
"My head is in the shed" -
I wish mine was.

I will photograph huts
and empty chairs, until I find mine.
I tried an upturned bucket
By the milky elbow river -
but hours of flight away.
I borrowed a jetty at Nimpo lake,
It moved with the water
and I ached with the beauty -
until the owners came.

It is like looking for
Somewhere to be buried
Somewhere to be married
Somewhere to live.

There is a chair
In an old shed with
a fire and a stream running through,
walls black from neglect,
seem cleaner as I sit
by the fire on the altar of my life -
It is a good chair
by a good fire
But it is inside.

There is somewhere
an outside inside shed with splinters,
A chair with cushions,
a window -
with a sea view
and an open door to heaven.

HEAVEN'S GATES AND OPEN HEAVENS

Land and territory, times and seasons are important in the kingdom. In some locations it seems easier to pray and easier to see healings and miracles released. Jacob had an encounter of the 'God kind' in one such place. In the midst of a journey he stopped for the night because it had gone dark, used a stone as a pillow and dreamt -

"He saw a stairway resting on the earth, with its top reaching heaven, and the angels of God were ascending and descending on it". God spoke to him about his destiny and his descendants. "When Jacob awoke from his sleep he thought, "Surely the Lord is in this place; and I was not aware of it". He was afraid and said, "How awesome is this place! This is none other than the house of God; this is the gate of heaven" (Genesis 28;12,16,17).

In the language of the Celtic Christians he had found a 'thin place' where the veil between heaven and earth was barely there. Jesus refers to this open heaven in John 1:51 - "I tell you the truth, you shall see heaven open and the angels of God ascending and descending on the Son of Man". The Celtic Christians wanted to separate themselves to an intense focus on God so they chose 'thin places', isolated and desolate places on cliffs, in forests and 'on the islands of the sea'.

The chapel of St. Govan's is wedged into the Pembrokeshire cliffs near Bosherton. Govan warned passing ships of the treacherous rocks around the headland and rescued and looked after shipwreck survivors.

 It might have been this and his fresh water supply that made him a target of pirates and wreckers. It is said that he hid from those who came to kill him in a crevice in the rock by his cell praying for God to save him. The rock is said to have closed around him and he out-waited the patience of his would-be killers.

Skellig Michael,

The most startling and extreme of the island monastic settlements is surely that of Skellig Michael, a ragged tooth of rock eight and a half miles off the Kerry coast of Ireland. The handful of beehive cells and the treacherous sea journey speak, even now, of an extreme devotion, carved out in discipline and framed in wild seas.

It is a struggle to get there by boat today, in a coracle it takes some imagining! It was probably founded by St. Suibhne in the sixth century and it was only in the eleventh century that the monks retreated to Ballyinskelligs on the mainland. These isolated retreats reveal lives abandoned to God's care in the face of raging elements and hostile forces - the Skelligs underwent Viking raids and St Govan was attacked by pirates.

It poses a question for us in the increasingly fragile, global environment of the twenty-first century. What does it mean for us to live out the reality of God as a safe place in the midst of extremity? Maybe true safety is found only in connection with Him, as from that place we find courage to risk and courage to truly live.

Yet, many of us fear that if we spend time with Jesus it will be a waste of time. We think He won't speak to us and if He does we think we're making it up! John 10:2-5 speaks directly into this.

" The man who enters by the gate is the shepherd of His sheep. The watchman opens the gate for Him, and the sheep listen to His voice. He calls his own sheep by name and leads them out. When He has brought out all His own He goes on ahead of them, and His sheep follow Him because they know His voice. But, they will never follow a stranger, in fact they will run away from Him because they do not recognise a strangers voice".

We may think he never speaks to us or that we can't hear Him. Yet, we hear him more frequently than we believe. He drew us, spoke to us, convicted us when we first came to faith. We mostly know when an action or a thought is not good. Sometimes a person or a situation comes to mind and we know that we need to pray, these are just a few examples of Him speaking.

His voice is normally an inner voice, although at times people do hear an audible voice. The inner voice can sound like our own thought life. "It is as though someone is talking directly to our minds from within ... we can learn how to recognize the Shepherd's voice as distinct from other tapes that are playing in our minds and hearts".[3]

We recognize His voice more easily the more we get to know Him, just as you easily recognise someone you know well even if you haven't spoken to them for a long time. We can test what he is saying from the Bible; we can test it by checking it out with others; by asking Jesus whether it is him or not; by the peace, or otherwise, the Holy Spirit who lives in us is giving; we can test it by the fruit that it produces in our lives.

There is a childlike trust and a childlike dependency in 'listening prayer'. A lot of it comes down to asking Him questions and listening to the answers. It means finding out what He thinks and feel. We can ask Him if He has adventures He wants to take us on: the adventure of finding Him in the meeting place He has already prepared in our own hearts, or the adventure of connection with others.

What does He want to say to you specifically, as you meditate (chew deeply, reflect) on this passage? - John 10:2-5.

You could ask him two questions - What does this mean and what should I do ?

Fear of failure or fear of rejection mean we will not ask, or will not expect Him to answer. Maybe it is time to be humble enough to believe that He is true to his word and that not only does He want to speak to us but that e will help us to listen to Him. There is simplicity in the expectancy that he wants to speak and that we can hear; it means being vulnerable enough to give it a go.

He is calling us to a deeper knowing of Him, in past times it has been called contemplative prayer, the rich treasure the Christian mystics spent their lives upon. It is the beholding bliss of His gaze, the face to face encounter, the kindness of His eyes, the exchange of His molten love and glory.

Our heart is a meeting place with Him, He lives in us - "I pray that out of his glorious riches He may strengthen you with power through His Spirit in your inner being, so that Christ may dwell in your hearts through faith" (Ephesians 3:16-17).

The journey to the meeting place of the heart, the place of His presence within, is the most incredible adventure I have experienced. It has been a journey over the last five years through changing inner landscapes into the unfolding rooms of the Father's house . It started as a prayer for healing and as a desire for more of Him. I find it is becoming a place to live rather than somewhere to go on day trips. It seems that even people like myself who don't find prayer easy can learn what it is to "dwell in the house of the Lord for ever".

The first place He showed me was my heart as a tumbled down Welsh cottage, walls blackened by years of neglect but with a fire and a stream running through, and a chair where I could sit with Him.

The mystics over the ages in the Christian Church had grander visions but the same starting place - He makes His home in our hearts.

"Let us realize that we have within us a most splendid palace built entirely of gold and precious stones ... there is no structure so beautiful as a soul filled with virtues ... this palace dwells the Mighty King who has deigned to become your Father, and Who is seated on a throne of priceless value - by which I mean your heart" (Teresa of Avila).[6]

"And I was still awake, and then our lord opened my spiritual eyes and showed me my soul in the middle of my heart. I saw my soul as large as if it were a kingdom; and from the properties that I saw in it, it seemed to me to be a glorious city. In the centre of that city sits our Lord Jesus, true God and true man glorious, highest Lord; and I saw him dressed imposingly with glory" (Julian of Norwich).[7]

The Father is committed to forging a safe place within; a depth of relationship which makes it safe to move out and adventure into his universe, into the dangerous places of our world and our lives. At times it feel like the cautious stepping out of a shy toddler born to explore yet frightened in case separation from a safe person means abandonment and death. He becomes our safe place as He makes his home in us and as we know safety within we can release the possibility of that to others. The meeting place of the heart becomes a gateway to adventure through intimacy in Him. The adventures may be in the supernatural realm, or in the everyday but it is in this place, which no human being can fill that we encounter Him.

CONNECT WITH CONTEMPLATIVE PRAYER.

"One thing I ask of the Lord, this is what I seek: that I may dwell in the house of the Lord all the days of my life, to gaze upon the beauty of the Lord and to seek Him in His temple"(Psalm 27:4).

It is beholding and being held, it is, at times, beyond words. It can start with an outpouring of emotion to God. It often ends, or maybe begins, when we get overwhelmed by His love. It is heart to heart and spirit to spirit.

HOW DO WE GET THERE?

• Choose a passage from the Bible, maybe in this instance part of Psalm 27 - remembering that a purpose of the words in the Bible is to lead us to the One whose book it is!
• Read over it reflectively, slowly.
• When a short phrase grabs you turn it into prayer.
• Move beyond words into wordless or nearly wordless prayer.
• You may find yourself gazing on/ beholding Jesus
• After you have finished it may help to journal - write down what happened- this can be an aid to further reflection.

IT'S HARD TO CONCENTRATE - HELP!

• Find a place on your own where it is quiet and you won't be disturbed.
• Give yourself time it can take a while to switch off to everything that has been going on.
• If that's difficult write a 'to do' list for later.
• Give Him the things you are anxious about.
• Confess any sin.
• Choose His will, refuse the will of the enemy.
• Call your mind into line say 'no' to random thoughts.
• Focus on Jesus. If still stuck worship, pray in tongues for a bit until you feel more connected.
• Ask Him to show you what the block is and how He wants to deal with it!

Prayer becomes a journey of encounter and intimacy, a time and place of meeting with the indwelling spirit of Christ. What does it look like when He makes His home with us?

John 14:2, "In my Father's house are many rooms; if it were not so I would have told you, I am going there to prepare a place for you", can be a living reality now, as well as a place of future fulfilment.

Brad Jersak helped frame some of what we were already encountering in his book "Can you Hear Me?" This is a listening prayer exercise from "Can you hear Me?" that has helped loads of people find their way into the meeting place of the heart.

CONNECT WITH THE MEETING PLACE

- Ask Jesus, "You have created within my heart a dwelling place for Your presence. Would You now show me that place? Would You now meet with me there?

- As He begins to reveal such a meeting place in your heart, step into it by faith. Find the Lord there and welcome him. Draw near to Hm and He will draw near to you.

- Gaze on Him, listen to Him, invite Him to hold you.

- Resist every distraction and remove every block that would hinder such communion. Seek this pearl of the kingdom with all your heart. You will find it. Ask for it and you will receive it.

- Then move in for good. Live with Him and in Him forever. This is the promise of the Meeting Place".

(Brad Jersak)

BLOG - FATHER'S HOUSE

www.blog

"Saw inner landscape - a landscape of desert desolation, desert of my heart: Desolation within, desolation without. Utter destruction burnt ground - wild fire has burnt me - 'Can these bones live?' Jesus standing silent in the midst of it - pain, intense, no words, draws me also into silence. Perhaps my draw to wilderness and wasted landscape is because of the inner echo. And there is beauty in it. The marshlands, mysterious channels, amidst the green and the mud flats, textured, gleaming, etched and patterned in tide ... Lie down in His presence ask Him to touch the desert in me ... He walks with me in the desolate no- hope- for- future place and it seems that a path opens up. He said to me - "You like adventures". Today I feel too fragile for them but inside I am willing. It seems hope may be seeing myself as He sees me...maybe the desert leads somewhere.

In the desert ask him to show me what He sees... the desert place is the beginning of a well with golden water flowing, beautiful gardens, different landscapes behind the different doors, the desert leading to the green place. I seem small, lost almost, until I know He is with me. He is with me in the desert and leads me out into a year in the "green place".

The green place is Psalm 23 to me. Wrecked I ask Him to heal my wounds in "the midst of my enemies" - my sin and my wrong belief. And I experience and know to the very depths, the power and completeness of the cross and the strength of the blood of Jesus ... Then He takes me to slowly climb and explore the mountain from which His presence flows to the people and places of least resistance. Leave the shepherd's cottage huddled close onto the wall of the Fathers house and find that I too can make my home with Him. He will not reject me. There is much to explore.

The journey to the safe place, to the place of His presence - of deep connection - childish games, a cuddle of acceptance have been part of a discovery of the Father's House in me. It is also great riches, landscapes that change...rooms that unfold and are still unfolding.

Promise Room - a Rainbow Room like a huge cathedral - so high arches and so vast sky. Soak in multicoloured grace and rest in promise. Map room, hidden peoples, forgotten peoples, his world map like illuminated glass in curious relief and incredible beauty - a small room- do many go there? Treasures from darkness room - a room with no shame - a depth of love beyond telling and the Healing rooms, the Garden ... so much.

As I reflect on this I see there has been a journey through the Psalms over these last years. Psalm 22 - the Psalm of Crucifixion, Psalm 23 - the Green Place, Psalm 24 - Ascend the Hill of the Lord. As we meet Him in Scripture, He can also lead us to the meeting place of the heart. He can meet us in our memories. He simply wants to meet with us.

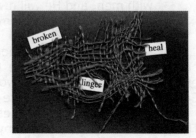

GO DEEPER

THE FATHER'S HOUSE

"Let not your heart be troubled; you believe in God, believe also in Me. In My Father's house are many mansions (dwelling places); if it were not so, I would have told you. I go to prepare a place for you. And if I go and prepare a place for you, I will come again and receive you to Myself; that where I am, there you may be also. And where I go you know, and the way you know." John 14:1-4

The meaning of Jesus' words to His disciples on the night that He was betrayed have been fought over for centuries in order to support one doctrine or another. Does He mean His return after the resurrection or an end-time conclusion of all things? The simplest answer is to not let our heart be troubled, to believe in God and believe also in Jesus. The amazing thing about Jesus' words is that they can speak to us on so many different levels. Yes, there is a victorious return in the resurrection, there is also a place prepared for us in heaven that Jesus comes to take us to at the end of our life, or at the end of the age. But there is a deeper whole bible context truth that is contained here alongside this, that God the Father, through the Son prepares a dwelling place for us, an inheritance given, where He desires to be with us. This is His heart for us, here are a few examples:

1. Adam and Eve in the Garden - a well defined prepared dwelling place.
2. Noah and the Ark, God invites him in to the many-roomed, prepared place, and means of salvation.
3. Abraham's promise of a land for his descendants to dwell in
4. Joseph's confession to his brothers that God had turned their evil into good and prepared a place for the sons of Israel to dwell.
5. The Exodus story is all about God taking his people to a prepared and promised l and of Sabbath rest, wherein they would dwell and He would be their God.
6. During the Exile in captivity the promise came time and again of a return and re-inhabiting of the land. Central to this is preparing a way for the coming King
7. All of this is finally summed up at the end time gathering and the new Jerusalem, where a voice in heaven declares "Behold, the tabernacle of God is with men, and He will dwell with them, and they shall be His people. God Himself will be with them and be their God." Revelation 21:3

The Greek noun 'mone' variously translated 'mansions', 'rooms' and 'dwelling places', only occurs once again in the NT, and in this very same chapter, 14:23. Here Jesus promises those who keep his word that the Father will love him and both the Father and Son 'will come to him and make Our home (mone) with him'.

Further Jesus tells his disciples that they know the way to this place where He is going. The first meaning is evidenced by his reply in 14:6 that He is the way the truth and the life and the only way to the Father. We will only gain access to our heavenly home through him and his sacrifice on the cross, there is no other way. And yet there is so much more here about the daily living out of our faith that we could miss if we just remain with these as proof texts regarding Jesus exclusive claim as Saviour of mankind. Yes Jesus is the only way to the Father, in Him is truth and life. But let's look further at what he is saying:

- He's saying that there is a way to the Father's house,

- And that a dwelling is being prepared for them

- That they know the way to the Father's house

- They know the way because they know Him who is the Way (6)

- We already know the Father because we know Jesus the Son (7, 9)

- That Jesus and the Father are perfectly united, and because He is going to the Father's house, untold blessings will be released (10-14).

So there is a present reality to all this and not only an eschatological (end-time) fulfilment. And to confirm this Jesus immediately speaks of the coming Spirit who will enable this abiding in Him and keeping of His commandments. Indeed there is the assurance in 14:18 that He 'will not leave you orphans (literally 'fatherless'); I will come to you'.

At this point a crucial clarification is introduced by a disciples question (14:22), 'How is it that you will be made known (Greek 'emphanizo' from which we get the English words 'emphasis' and 'emphatic') to us but the world won't know or see you?'

The answer is contained in the earth-shattering promise in verse 23, that if we love Him and keep His word, then the very Godhead will come and make His dwelling place (mone) with us. Here Jesus turns the image of the Father's house right around. Whereas previously He spoke of a place for us to go to, now the Father's home is within us.

This truth will be applied to us by the Comforter, the Holy Spirit, making us no longer orphans by indwelling us, teaching us all things, and reminding us of Jesus. Again Jesus tells His disciples not to let their heart be troubled or afraid, for when these things come to pass we will believe.

So the indwelling emphatic reality of the Father, Son and Spirit making Their home in us, is the means by which we are made no longer orphans, troubled hearts are made peaceful and the perfect love of the Father casts out all fear. This is then the place we are to choose to live and remain, this Father's house within us.

Hywel Rhys Edwards

41

CONNECT WITH HIM IN SCRIPTURE

Choose a Gospel story and imagine yourself in that biblical scene. What can you hear, see, smell, sense/feel. What is Jesus saying to you through that story? Open the eyes of your heart. Pause and ask yourself how you feel at particular points in the story. Let the Holy Spirit lead you. In the Gospel story below imagine yourself there too. Pause and ask yourself the questions as you go through the story. Allow Jesus to come and meet you in a very real, fresh way today.

John 21 v.1-13:
After the resurrection, Jesus appears to the disciples.
Imagine you are there too with the disciples.
You are down by the sea with the disciples with Simon Peter, Thomas, Nathanael, the sons of Zebedee and two others.
Simon Peter says I'm going out to fish and you say we'll go with you. So you all get into the boat. What do you see? Have a look around you. Feel the motion of the boat and the gentle breeze on your face. You are out on the boat till dark, but you catch nothing.

How do you feel? What are the disciples feeling?

Early in the morning, Jesus is standing on the shore, but you and the other disciples don't realise who it is. Jesus calls out to you, "Friends haven't you any fish?"
"No", you call back.
He says, "Throw your net on the right side of the boat and you will find some".

What do you feel about His suggestion?
How are you feeling, what can you see?

When you do what Jesus suggested, you are unable to haul the net in because of the large number of fish.
How do you feel now? What does it look like to see all those fish come in?
Then the disciple whom Jesus loved said to Peter, "It is the Lord!"
When you look at Jesus now, looking into His eyes, how has his appearance changed to you?
Simon Peter leaped into the water to greet Jesus. The others followed in the boat, towing the net full of fish.

Where are you now, as you go to meet Jesus?

When you reach the shore, you see a fire of burning coals there with fish on it, and some bread. Take in the smell of the fish cooking, see the bread waiting for you. Feel the warmth of the fire against your skin, warming you up at breakfast time. Hear the fire crackling.

Jesus says to you, "Bring some of the fish you have caught". Simon Peter climbs aboard the boat and drags the net ashore. It was full of large fish, 153, but even with so many the net was not torn. How do you feel as you see the large number of fish? What is the mood of the disciples now. Look at the net, bulging, but not torn.

Jesus says to you, "Come and have breakfast".
Jesus is close to you now. Look at His face, clothes. How is He looking at you? What are you thinking?

None of you dare ask him, "Who are you?" You know it is the Lord.

Rest in that feeling of knowing it is Jesus.
Jesus takes the bread, breaks it and gives it to you, and does the same with the fish.
Does Jesus say anything to you?
What do you want to say to Him?
As you sit by the fire, how close by is Jesus?
Sit and have a chat to Him now.

Zoe Britnell

QUOTE
"At times (you) touch a state of inward silence…
at this time to pray out loud, or in any conventional way would only draw you away from an inward experience and draw you back to an outward surface prayer…But if you do not speak, what shall you do? Nothing? Simply yield to the inward drawing".
Madame Guyon[4]

"With face turned to heaven, and hands and eyes lifted to God, in complete surrender and with the warmest devotion, he prayed saying 'My God, my all'. These words he groaned to God with copious tears, again and again with solemn devotion until dawn: 'My God, my all' and no more".
St Francis by Bernard[5]

CONNECT - UNPACK YOUR RUCKSACK IN THE FATHER'S HOUSE

Key Scripture : John 14:2

"In my Father's house there are many rooms; if it were not so I would have told you.
I am going to prepare a place for you."

This exercise is a way of allowing Jesus to meet with you over everyday stuff you carry around. Ask the Holy Spirit to help you and show you all that you need to know. You could do this in whatever way you choose, ask Him direct, or you could use this exercise to spark your imagination.

Imagine you are holding a rucksack, what is in it? What do these things symbolise for you? For example -
- Cheque book and credit card - could represent your financial worries, debt problems
- Diary - could represent your work commitments, meetings and busy schedule
- Make-up bag - could represent your self-image, how you feel about yourself
- Aspirin - could represent the things that cause you pain and how you deal with them
- Keys - could represent your roles and responsibilities as mother, father, son, daughter, leader, manager, caretaker, secretary.
- Bible - could represent your relationship with God - what state is it in?

It's good to give all this stuff we carry around to Jesus.

Find a quiet and comfortable place to sit or lie down. Close your eyes and invite the Holy Spirit to come closer and help you. Maybe you will see yourself at the bottom of a path that leads up to your Heavenly Father's house.

As you start to walk up the path, feel the gravel beneath your feet, a soft breeze brushes past your face and you smell the scent of the flowers dancing in the breeze. You are coming closer to the front door, and as you approach the door, you notice it is open. As you stand before the door about to enter the Father's House, how does it feel? You push the door open and step into the Father's house, Jesus is in the room, where is He?

As you look around the meeting room what do you see, what is the room like? Jesus gestures for you to join Him on the sofa, you and He sit next to each other and you begin to unpack your rucksack. As you take each item out and hand it to Him, Tell Him how you feel about it and then pause and wait for Him to speak to you about each one. What does He want you to see or hear? Stay there with Him for as long as you are able and give Him space to speak, ask Him what He thinks and feels about each one.

Once you're done, write about what you experienced, there may still be more He wants you to know!

Deb Chapman

GO DEEPER - The Inner Meeting Place of the Heart

Then God said, "Let Us make man in Our image, according to Our likeness; let them have dominion over the fish of the sea, over the birds of the air, and over the cattle, over all the earth and over every creeping thing that creeps on the earth" (Gen 1:26). In the first three verses of the Bible we see the threefold God at work in perfect union. The Father, the creator, made heaven and earth. The Spirit of God is hovering or brooding over the waters, ready for action. The Son, being the Word of God, is the means by which things are created, God spoke and it came into being (see John 1:23, All things were made through Him, and without Him nothing was made that was made). So we see here an expression that is consistent throughout the Bible, of the inter-relationship of God, Father, Son and Holy Spirit. The perfect love and unity they share then bursts out in the creative act of forming man and woman, out of the dust of the earth, in His very image and likeness.

The circle of relationship is extended to include man with the plan that together with the Father, Son and Spirit, he should bring in God's kingdom rule on the earth. We were created with this specific purpose, and with the nature of this unity and love inbuilt.Yes this creative purpose and image was marred at the fall, and throughout the generations from Adam to today. However, in Christ there is a new creation, the old has gone the new has come. So the original creative purpose of God is restored.

We again have inbuilt the potential for this perfect unity and love with the Godhead, and to work out his purposes on earth. The creation story shows man being placed in a garden to which God would come in the cool of the evening to enjoy each other's company (Gen 3:8). This was the first meeting place of God and man. Interestingly it reflects Paul's assertion that God has a life of good works for us that he has specifically created us for (Ephesians 2:10), and that He seeks to meet and partner with us in the walking out of our purpose.In a real sense God is with us at each step of our journey (Matthew 28:20), but there is also an intimate inner meeting place that He has for us.

This inner meeting place will also reflect this Trinity that made us in His likeness. At times we will meet the Father, the Creator, and interact as a child of His promise. We will be included in His plans and involved in His creativity. Another time we will meet the Son, as our brother and Saviour, as our King and Lord, healer and friend. At this point the list of His names serve to inspire us to explore the richness of relationship with Him. And the Spirit will also meet with us to bring us into all truth, reveal the glory of the Father and Son, to empower and equip us. Much of what we've seen about our entering in to the heavenly places and being seated with Him is also the way in which we enter that place of intimacy with Him. Whereas the adventures in the heavenlies reflect our inheritance, and are a lost part of how we are to fulfil the commission to fill all creation and subdue it; the inner meeting place is more about the relationship that God intended for us from the beginning. Both aspects are required.

Built into our ability to be fruitful and multiply is the necessity for intimacy. So let us draw near to God, and He will draw near to us (James 4:4), and let us enter boldly into His presence by the new and living way (Hebrews 4:14-16; 10:19-22).But what sort of meeting place can we expect?

It could be said that the possibilities are endless, which is a good thing with eternity stretching out before and behind us! Think of some of the names of God and how we can meet him in each of these reflections of His nature:

YHWH - I am that I am; the name by which He made himself known to Moses.

YHWH Yireh - The Lord sees, Genesis 22:14.

YHWH Nissi - The Lord my banner, Exodus 17:15.

YHWH Shalom - The Lord my peace, Judges 6:24.

And the names that his people gave him reflecting their meeting with him:

Shepherd - Psalm 23; Isaiah 40.

Fortress - 2 Samuel 22:2; Psalm 31:3; Proverbs 18:10.

Redeemer - Job 19:25; Psalm 19:14.

Healer - Exodus 15:26; Psalm 103:3.

Saviour - 2 Samuel 22:3; Luke 1:47.

In Micah 4:1-4 we read of God's redemptive plan for us, in which He portrays us as sitting each under his own vine and fig tree (place of fruitfulness) and walking in the name of the Lord. This could be interpreted as keeping commandments, but in the light of the New Testament where we read of walking and living in the light (Ephesians 5:8; 1 John 1: 7; 2:10), there is room to see here a walk of intimacy in the very names of God.

An example of such a life would be Abraham's walk with the Lord, another would be David. Psalm 16 reveals how David lived his life out of this inner meeting place, it is a good place to meditate on what it means to keep the Lord always before me. The supreme example of this inner meeting place is of course Jesus. In Mathew, Mark and Luke we read often of Him seeking solitude from the crowd in order to pray and commune with the Father. Yet this is seen on another level in John, wHere there is a much more intimate and immediate knowing between Father and Son, look up the occasions where Jesus calls on His Father before men, and speaks of only doing and saying what He sees and hears the Father doing: John 5:19-20, 30; 6:46, 56-57; 8:28-29, 38.

Then in John 10 Jesus unfolds His name as the Good Shepherd, and leads us all into that same place of intimacy with Himself as He enjoys with the Father. John 15 reveals the abiding or remaining in that place that is essential for our fruitfulness. Back to the Garden, and in chapter 3 where we read of God walking in the garden in the cool of the evening, Adam and Eve are found by Him hiding because of their shame and sin. Where God intended them to enjoy that meeting place with them, they allowed fear to drive them away. As this place of inner meeting is restored to us in Jesus, let us learn to seek Him there, and learn to recognise His voice and time of visitation with us.

Hywel Rhys Edwards

WALK THE LAND,
CARRY HIS PRESENCE

WALK THE LAND, CARRY HIS PRESENCE

"WALKING IN HUMILITY, COUNTER-CULTURE, NO PLANS,
NO PROGRAMME BUT CERTAIN HE WILL LEAD -
TIME FOR PEOPLE, TIME TO LISTEN, TIME TO PRAY.
TEAMS FLOWING ACROSS THE LAND, SHOWING THE
KINDNESS OF THE FATHER'S HEART. SEEKING
OUT THE POOR - SALVATIONS AND HEALING
BREAKING OUT".

As we live a life focused on Jesus, as we "waste time" on Him we are more prepared to "waste time" on others. We have less need to be in control of each moment of our lives. We are prepared to be led by the Holy Spirit rather than our own agendas. It looks like doing the stuff that Jesus did, wanting to do only what He saw the Father doing.

It means getting wet, feeling foolish.
It means confronting empty streets and empty eyes.
It means feeling a constant outsider, waiting to be given an invitation to connect.
It means giving an invitation to connect.
It means living rejection's sting and mockery.
It means welcoming people home.
It means having a generous, hospitable heart
It means hope breaking out where there was none.
It means seeing someone healed in front of your eyes.
It means being a touchable answer to a desperate prayer.
It means being a living demonstration that He is good and that He cares.
It means being threatened and being a threat to the way things are.
It means living whatever you have known Him to be for you in the wildness of his multicoloured grace.
It means receiving as much as giving.
It means being in need more than wanting to be needed.
It means laying down power for his power to be revealed.

"Walk the Land" is revolution, it is the rebuilding of community in many acts of kindness, in signs and wonders, it is about welcoming the angels.

It is the powerlessness of choosing His power rather than the power of the world's systems. It values that which is worth valuing in a culture and values that which is unvalued in the face of that which is worshipped.

It connects with our Celtic roots and makes Jesus accessible, immediate and available in an uninhibited way. In our bureaucratic, 'Roman' society, where welfare and help is primarily controlled by central government, where communities as sources of life and empowerment have all but broken down, the availability of help for those in need is determined by the ability to complete forms and answer questions correctly. It is about whether you live in a deprived area and whether or not you fit the criteria. Sadly many of our churches are shaped by these prevailing norms - evangelism is seen as someone else's responsibility and there is a programme to hide behind.

Compassion burns within, the flame, a revolution of hope, a belief that the darkest and most ravaged of situations can break out in resurrection. It is subversive, harasses an acceptance of numbed pain, the consequence of sin both personal and structural. It refuses the pull of Christendom and Empire.

Pilgrimage is lived out of passion. It is "lets go walkabout" in the Holy Spirit. Walking the land, carrying His presence is an intentional desire to overspill, flow out with the wonders of God. It is about carrying the overshadowing of His Spirit within us amongst the pain of the marginalised. It is about the rhythm of our lives taking us into the streets and alleys the "no go" areas of our communities and nations.

Jesus walked. We mostly don't walk much. In our world, walking can mean meeting and having time to "waste" on those who are less empowered, the elderly, mums with small children, the young, the sick and the unemployed.

IT MEANS SEEING

BLOG

I was with two young people walking in Llanelli and as we were walking I felt God say to look out for a mum with a baby in a pushchair - not difficult! But 45 minutes later no sign of woman or baby! We carried on walking and one of my friends saw up ahead a woman with a child in a pushchair. That was my cue - we three headed towards her trying to be casual and not frighten her!

I introduced us and explained that we offering to pray for people if they had any health issues or worries. She declined saying that she attended the Church in Wales. We talked some more and I listened to her story of mental illness and alcoholic partner. She told me how she would sit on her back step and pray for help most days - I told her that Jesus had sent us to her today and that He had told me to look out for a woman pushing a child in a pushchair. Her eyes brightened with the realisation that He knew, He heard, He cared. We prayed for her and for her family and I gave her a contact number should she need help or someone to talk to. We agreed to stop talking before we both cried.

Whilst I was talking to the woman one of my friends was talking to the young boy in the pushchair. He was wary at first but once sure of her was hungry for connection with her eyes and to hold her hands, not letting go. She was moved to tears and deeply impacted by the depth of the need she saw. If we hadn't walked there would have been no connections.

Deb Chapman

BLOG

Walk the Land is time to waste on people. It feels like a privilege to spend time listening to someone tell their story, hearing their pain and struggle; walking alongside them for five or ten minutes in their journey, standing with them on their side of the wall.

The simple act of listening - proper listening, not the half-glazed state of being somewhere else in your head - is hard work but rewarded with a connection that breaks their isolation. Then, from there to pray for them, asking the Holy Spirit to pour out the love and kindness of Jesus into their lives, heal their pain, their body, their wounded heart.

Walk the Land is walking with humanity.

Deb Chapman

Our eyes long for connection, yet cannot bare the raw gaze - judging us, undressing us, consuming us - consumer items - wanted not wanted, desired not desired. The turned back of rejection is painful. The pain of not being seen is even greater. Eyes are desperate to connect yet fear it as much as life.

As we walk, value the touch of His glory in every broken form and ravaged face, we recognize Him. The longing to be known can only be fully met in Him. This is not sick sentimentality that refuses to wash grace in truth but the rawness of beauty and ugliness, futility and purpose, the abuser and the abused. These are lives where demons feed and feast unhindered - lives that are stark cries of pain - yet wordless. The smell of those covered in shit and sick with no place or desire to wash, to be acceptable - it is all here.

Jesus walked, saw and welcomed. "As Jesus was walking beside the Sea of Galilee, he saw two brothers Simon called Peter and his brother Andrew, they were casting a net into the lake, for they were fishermen, "Come follow Me" Jesus said", and I will make you fishers of men." At once they left their nets and followed him (Matthew 4;18-20).

In walking we slow down, have an opportunity to connect, not only with the environment we are walking, but to really see. Jesus saw who these men were, the destiny on their lives. He didn't see lack of education and current commitments as an issue- he saw the possibilities and the Father's thumbprint on their lives.

Is this how we see? Do we see through the Father's eyes the ones who will abandon themselves to His Son?

Reflection -
- What do we see when we walk down the street?
- Who do we see?
- What do they see in our eyes? Recognition, kindness, do they know they have been truly seen and valued - loved and not discarded? Have they seen the eyes of Jesus with all the unexpectedness of His responses, the unusual questions?

Go out and make connection with the people He is showing you. You can call it looking for "divine appointments" or simply seeing the ones He wants you to see.

The first walk in scripture was a walk of intimacy, walking with the Father in the cool of the day. Jesus walked everywhere. He walked Galilee a place He knew and loved so that those who walked in darkness could see a great light. As He walked revelation broke into desperate lives, miracles and healings brought life, the hungry were fed and the dead raised. In His humanity, the need for food and water gave rise to more miracles as the welcome He received released more revelation and more miracles.

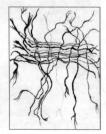

God leads us to the places He loves, so He can lead us to the people He loves. Galilee was a loved place and as we walk we can be people with hospitable hearts generous, nurturing dreams and the dreamers who carry them.

To walk is faith in action - lived-out trust born in the place of intimacy and demonstrated in the ordinary decisions and choices of the day. Walking the land, carrying His presence simplifies the complexity of our lives to a raw baseline. It focuses us on the essentials of what Jesus did and what He wants to be for us today.

Do we notice when someone has reached out to touch Him, or are we focused on more important destinations? "Where ever you are - be there!" can become more than a cliché. It is a parable in which we have nothing to rely on except Him and His leading. It is "walking as He walked" amidst an over-laden culture. It calls us to evaluate what we really need in our lives with our families, in our workplace, in our communities. It is a magnifying glass turning the sun's great fire upon crumpled paper to light dry sticks. Was it always like this? Jesus regarded as a scrounger, a need-meeter - someone with eyes to see the child behind the burnt-out adult pain.

THE POWER OF JOY

"Inebriated holy joy" - we can see joy break out around us in broken lives and traumatised communities. A joy released which gives the strength to build and to live again. This can sound very religious but the heart of it is as simple as being really glad to see someone, letting them know that they have lit up your day. Community transformation, joy by joy?!

remember joy

"The Spirit of the Sovereign Lord is on me, because He has anointed me to preach good news to the poor. He has sent me to proclaim freedom for the prisoners and recovery of sight for the blind, to release the oppressed, to proclaim the year of the Lord's favour".
Luke 4:18-19

"I will turn their mourning into gladness; I will give them comfort and joy instead of sorrow".
Jeremiah 31:13b

In a child's first two years, the desire to experience joy in loving relationships is the most powerful force in life. In fact some neurologists now say that the basic human need is to be the "sparkle in someone's eye"... When this joy is the strongest force in a child's world, life makes sense, because children look forward to moments when they can reconnect to joy - being with their beloved... Life makes sense and is empowered by joy when people are in relationship with those who love them and are sincerely "glad to be with them". Because joy is relational, it is also a contagious experience. Joy is produced when someone is "glad to see me", which stirs up a bit of joy in me. Then my joy is returned and the giver's joy is increased as well. Joy also comes from being in relationship with God. Through the Bible it is established that a powerful joy comes from a relationship with God who knows everything about me and is still "as-glad-as-glad-can get" to be with me.[1]

CONNECT - BUILDING JOY

Building joy means getting closer to God and to people. While it is a very authentic process that cannot be fabricated, here are some "joy building" ideas to first practice with our families and then to extend to the wounded community.

- Smile whenever you greet those you love, and use sincere voice tones.

- Ask questions that invite others to tell you truthfully how they are doing.

- Take a sincere interest in really knowing the other person. Work hard to understand the other's fears, joys, passions, talents and pain.

- Treat each other with dignity and respect. When ending a discussion, try to make both people feel affirmed.

- Use touch whenever appropriate: Hold hands, link arms, give hugs, and use physical connection as effectively as you can.

- Discover what brings the person joy: a time to talk, encouraging notes, a helping hand, or evening walks. Custom-fit your attempts to bring joy.

- Give them little surprises that will cause their eyes to light up, and let your eyes light up, too! The joy builds as the glances go back and forth.

- Cherish babies and children by establishing through words and actions that you are authentically "glad to be with them."[2]

Counter-culture, time to listen, to see people for their own sakes...

Buy flowers as we enter one village, the choice of colour seems important, wander round feeling foolish, looking for someone, anyone to whom they might belong! At point of deciding it was the wrong idea, see a mother and daughter. She was shaken, the week before she said that no one ever gave her flowers. In giving them said that Jesus appreciated all the unseen things she did in giving so much yet receiving so little back. He touched her in the midst of her depression, the flowers were her favourite colours, she had no connection with Christians or church, was shocked that God knew her and cared for her in such detail - I think I was too in the midst of my haphazard hearing and blundering around.

Later in the day we cause a panic alarm to be set off in an old people's home, then frighten them with our singing! Get propositioned by an elderly hairdresser and borrow a saucepan to brew up on a council estate. The saucepan in our need, becomes an opportunity to connect with an overwhelmed single parent struggling with depression. A friend who had two stillborn babies is able to comfort someone on drugs whose partner is again on the verge of miscarriage.

We pray for a man sick with heart problems, who a couple of months earlier had become a Christian through people we know in another part of the country. He wasn't sure if Jesus cared for him in his sickness, the meeting of friend of friends in an obscure place miles from his home, seemed to help, seemed to show that God hadn't forgotten him...

Try to find a place to sleep. It is not easy! We hadn't been invited into a home, so sleep rough in an old wood, on a bed of flowers and fears. We are not very brave so the angels come close as the witchcraft, the ancient rites and rituals, still active, are challenged in what becomes, a restful watch.

The sweetness of His presence, the touch of His face, is not sentiment but a deep cry. The woods a reminder of Gethsemene and the Cross where the tearing of his mind and body broke the darkest tortures and rituals of all mankind. A skylark rolls out of the sky with the dawn and dogs walk their owners in a valley barely touched by past revivals.

I like the way St Francis clowned around the place with his friends enjoying Jesus in the moment, laughing, being outrageous", inebriated with holy joy".[3] Happening miracles and tears, then drawing aside to reflect. Preaching to a hedgeful of sparrows and a man hiding behind the hedge giving several altar calls. Standing on his head to show a true perspective of Gods sustaining power, caring for lepers. This is not new stuff, it's the stuff of Jesus, the stuff of the gospels. This becoming as little children speaks of finding a sense of wonder, and the grace to play, to experiment, to risk, to create beyond the confines of an uptight religious mind. Hearing Him and finding a safe place in Him to adventure out from seems important for those of us who do cowardice well.

Jesus liked to walk, to connect with people and He liked to pray in lonely places; both sound good. "Yet the news about him spread all the more, so that crowds of people came to hear him and to be healed of their sicknesses. But Jesus often withdrew to lonely places and prayed" (Luke 5;15,16). Both sound good to me.

Jesus liked to walk...

CONNECT - DO 'WALK THE LAND AND CARRY HIS PRESENCE.'

Walk the land...ask the Holy Spirit what to do, where to go.... do whatever He shows you...Take bags of food around a poor estate...give to whoever He shows you...put in the bag a note saying this food is just a gift to show God is good...spend some time with them...give them a flyer with details on the back saying who Jesus is and that He wants to really meet them for the first time...Ask someone for their help, a drink of water, information - connect with being powerless, be the one in need... Give a bunch of flowers to someone to bring colour into their life...give a box of chocolates to someone else....a cup of hot chocolate on a cold day to another...an umbrella on a rainy day to someone else...Listen to someone, really listen and see what you learn....Say to someone else Jesus wants to heal them today...that He is still the same yesterday, today and forever...and see a miracle on the streets...Take a risk and go up to someone and ask them if there is anything they want prayer for...tell them that they have nothing to lose...see them open up about their family situation because they have had no-one else who would listen...see Jesus' light break into that darkness...

...Throw together a makeshift B-B-Q, accept all offers of help.

...See tears roll down a face, as they realise that someone loves them, and that He thinks they are beautiful...

...Bring a gift to a forgotten, poor estate...give it to someone who thinks the world has forgotten them....show them that He does care, and will go to the ends of the earth to show them kindness... that He will go to the places where no-one else will...

...Go to a town centre, lay out pictures on the floor (National Geographic do good ones)...let people come and see out of curiosity...explain to them that Jesus wants to speak to them today...ask them to pick 2 pictures, one that speaks to them of where they are at now, and one of where they would like to be, or just one that stands out to them...ask Jesus for a prophetic word into their situation...

...see them choose a picture that shows that they are bored,

...see them choose another that shows people partying as that is where they would like to be,

...ask Jesus to show them that He has the best party in the world for them,

...and a reason for living.

...see their face light up as they realise they have a purpose in life,

...see tears roll down their face,

...see Jesus in their face,

...see them meet Jesus face to face.

Zoe Britnell

56

"Jesus was the walking teacher. To join his mobile school you first had to obey the call to 'follow'. The Greek verb ('akoluthos') is made up of two parts, 'koluthos' means a path. So to follow Jesus literally meant to be on the same path as him. We can imagine Jesus sometimes teaching the twelve as he walked, more often just talking with two or three or even just one disciple. Sometimes there were crowds walking along with Jesus and it's likely that highlights of his teaching would have been relayed to people as they followed. We can picture people jostling for a place. On one of those occasions where large crowds were following him, Jesus stopped and turned round and the ranks gradually came to a halt and quieted down as he started to teach.

"If anyone comes to Me and does not hate his father and mother and his brother and sisters - yes even his own life - he cannot be my disciple" (Luke 14:26,27).

I can imagine myself in that crowd thinking, "Here I am walking after Jesus but am I following for the right motive? Am I just waiting for the next miracle? Am I really prepared to leave everything behind? Am I willing to take up the cross ready to suffer and die as I walk on the same path with Jesus?

Jesus used this strategy of walking - teaching to make disciples and it is also implied in the Great Commission itself where the verb "go" should more accurately be translated 'As you go on your way make disciples' ". David Pott [4]

Walking and teaching can become moments of revelation- memorably for the disciples returning to Emmaus after the death of their dreams. Jesus in his resurrected body joins them on the road - they finally recognise him when they break bread together. They said, "were our hearts not burning within us, while he talked with us on the road and opened the scriptures to us" (Luke 24: 32).

Dreams with tread on for rough terrain,
tough dreams,
No tough treading on our rough dreams

Walking the land carrying His presence is about moments of revelation breaking out. Often He speaks to us, often He opens the hearts of those we meet, sometimes it isn't words as much as action, being with someone in the midst of their pain. Sometimes it seems they literally experience the overshadowing of His presence through us.

CONNECT

• Go for a literal walk somewhere and ask Him to teach you whatever He chooses.

• A good way to connect with scripture is to imagine yourself in a biblical scene. Use your senses to connect. Ask questions. What did you hear, what did you see, what were you feeling? Join Jesus and the crowds in Luke 14 as He was walking, let Him ask you the question He asked them. Or allow Him to walk with you on the road to Emmaus in Luke24:13-35, what does He want to show you?

• Luke 24 v.13-35
[Jesus had been crucified and buried, and all the apostles had just been told that He was no longer in his tomb and were wondering what had happened].
 Now that same day two of them were going to a village called Emmaus, about seven miles from Jerusalem. They were talking with each other about everything that had happened.
Imagine that you are with them now and walking along that hot and dusty road.
As you talk and discuss these things with each other, Jesus himself comes up and walks along with you; but you were all kept from recognising HIm.
He asks you, "What are you discussing together as you walk along?"
You begin to tell him how you are feeling, about what has happened to Jesus.
You stand still with the others, with your faces downcast. One of them, named Cleopas, asks him, "Are you only a visitor to Jerusalem and do not know the things that have happened there in these days?"
"What things?" He asked.
"About Jesus of Nazareth," they replied. "He was a prophet, powerful in word and deed before God and all the people. The chief priests and our rulers handed Him over to be sentenced to death, and they crucified Him; but we had hoped that He was the one who was going to redeem Israel. And what is more, it is the third day since all this took place. In addition, some of our women amazed us. They went to the tomb early this morning but didn't find His body. They came and told us that they had seen a vision of angels, who said He was alive. Then some of our companions went to the tomb and found it just as the women had said, but Him they did not see."
How are you feeling at this point, the same as the others, disappointment, confusion, or do you feel differently? Is there a situation where you felt He was far away, or a situation where you didn't know if He was there at all? Do you need a fresh revelation of Him into a particular situation? Ask Him.
He said to them, "How foolish you are, and how slow of heart to believe all that the prophets have spoken! Did not the Christ have to suffer these things and then enter His glory?" And beginning with Moses and all the Prophets, He explains to you what was said in all the Scriptures concerning Himself.

What truth does Jesus want to speak into you now? What does He want you to see or hear or know?

As you approach the village to which you are going, Jesus acts as if He is going further. But you urge Him strongly, "Stay with us, for it is nearly evening; the day is almost over." So He goes to stay with you. When He was at the table with you, you watch Him as He takes the bread, gives thanks, breaks it and begins to give it to you all.

But then, all of a sudden, your eyes were opened and you recognize Him, but then he disappears from your sight.

How did Jesus look to you when you recognised Him? How do you feel now that He has gone from your sight?

You then turn and ask each other, "Were not our hearts burning within us while He talked with us on the road and opened the Scriptures to us?"

You then all get up and return at once to Jerusalem. You find the Eleven and those with them, meeting together, and tell them, "It is true! The Lord has risen and has appeared to Simon."

You then tell them what happened on the way, and how you recognized Jesus when He broke bread.

How do you feel as you tell the others about the encounter you have had with Jesus? Is there anything else Jesus wants to open your eyes to and reveal to you now?

Zoe Britnell

GO DEEPER

HOW DO WE WALK THE LAND AND CARRY HIS PRESENCE IN THE EVERYDAY?

For years I have heard sermons on evangelism, yet every word sidelines a large proportion of Christians because actually - they hate evangelism. It is promoted as a priority and we are made to feel guilty to motivate us, yet we secretly feel inadequate. The reality is an ideal put beyond the reach of the average guy. I have come up with all sorts of excuses myself and I meet Christians who had a vision of being a "Christian in the workplace" but fifteen years later, after mentioning Jesus once, haven't brought it up since. Evangelism is seen almost totally in terms of reaping, if you are not leading people to Christ instantly you are failing.

Yet you can only reap where there has been sowing and with a large proportion of the church feeling a failure it has reaped a different harvest - a barren wasteland of unplanted fields. It is time for a fresh approach to this issue, which will harness the workers so they can be in faith. I have often heard said when there is disappointment over the response, "At least we sowed some seeds." This is not the language of faith, it is fatalistic. We need a fresh injection of faith, faith that works, faith that is natural and "sowable".

We live in a small post-industrial town, our house is right behind the railway station.

When there is an international rugby match on in Cardiff we can hear the fans at the station singing - the Welsh- the national anthem, the Irish 'Cockles and Mussels' ... what a racket! There is so much hope and excitement in their voices! Hope has motivated them to spend money, get themselves all the way to Cardiff. Hope is a motivator. But if they knew their team was going to lose, would they be so motivated? Would it be worth the cost - would it be worth it?

The Message puts it like this :

"The fundamental fact of existence is that this trust in God, this faith, is the firm foundation under everything that makes life worth living. It's our handle on what we can't see. The act of faith is what distinguished our ancestors, set them above the crowd" (Hebrews 11:1-2).

Let's face it we want to know that our lives count for something, that we make a difference. Faith gives us the confidence to dream again - our lives are worth living even after changing 10,000 nappies, getting into debt, struggling to get a job, our lives passing faster by the day - there is a key to living our lives to the full. "He who sows sparingly will reap sparingly and he who sows bountifully will also reap bountifully" (2 Corinthians 9:6).

A farmer does not sow and come home at night and say to his wife, well at least I sowed a few seeds. He sows expecting a harvest, why sow otherwise. He plans for a harvest, prepares the ground, waters, protects. Would he bother if there was no chance of a result- I don't think so! Yet we have so lost sight of a result that we have become without hope - demotivated.

We must believe in the' God factor.' This needs to come by revelation. Revelation can come to us when we understand just what it is and how it works. Revealed truth rather than head knowledge of the truth unlocks faith in us, which stirs up hope, which motivates us to act.

In Matthew 16 Jesus asked the disciples who they thought He was, they could have made an educated guess, they could have worked it out from the heavy hints Jesus had given, but no. Then Peter says, "You are the Christ, the Son of the living God." Jesus says you did not get this through your head, it was revealed to you by God. Jesus goes on to say that He will build His church on this rock. What was the rock - Peter? Jesus? No not even on Jesus - it was on the revelation of Jesus that He would build His church. Revelation is the key. And it simply means - God has broken through for us to understand, the "Penny has dropped."

Before we were Christians so much did not make sense. After becoming a Christian it all starts to hang together, we finally get it! And I think that we can all get it for our workplace, our school, our everyday, becoming confident that Jesus is building His church through us.

I learned an important lesson through reading a book about Keith Green, (a Christian musician who had lots of kids and died in a plane crash). He was highly pushy with his friends about Jesus and they were reacting to him. One day he came home to his wife Melody and said, "I made a big mistake today, I tried to be the Holy Spirit today, I tried to convict my friends of sin". The Bible is clear, it is the Holy Spirit who has this job, not us. We sow we water but the harvest is His.

The Holy Spirit puts us in touch with the bigger picture. Our lives cease to be futile. FAITH MAKES LIFE WORTH LIVING. Living by Faith is for all of us.

We can understand, by revelation, that Christ is in us! In the process of someone becoming a believer they go through many events and circumstances that lead to a final revelation of Jesus and wanting Him in their life. This process can go on for years. Other than meeting Jesus, the most significant thing on the journey will be to meet a Christian. When they meet you, they are meeting Jesus. It especially helps if you believe that, it puts faith into the mix.

I met a builder acquaintance recently and I asked him about his family and we had a bit of a chat. I still didn't manage to get the whole Gospel story in, no scripture spouted from my mouth but I went away with my heart singing - I never feel more saved than when I witness. I believe that he was meeting Jesus - JESUS IS STRONG ENOUGH TO REACH OUT THROUGH ME. I have faith for this, I sow knowing that it is true. It doesn't matter to me that I was a link in the chain, Jesus in me had reached out and I believe it.

We carry Jesus in our lives, it is a lost truth and therefore lacks the strength of faith to see it outworked. When I walk into a shop I know that Jesus has walked in with me, even sitting next to someone puts them within reach of Jesus, and all the more if I believe it, believe that it creates a hunger in people.

I was in a gym changing room and someone who was obviously mentally ill was upset because his pound for the locker had been stolen - he had only turned his back for a second. The room was full of people yet no-one would help. I found myself thinking - give him a pound. Yet something held me back, then I found myself shouting in my head- give the guy a pound, what is the matter with you. I found myself trying to work out how I could get it back! - GIVE HIM A POUND IDIOT! And I did, and I saw it, revelation came, Jesus was there. Still didn't get a chance to preach - sorry! But I knew that I left a question in everyone's heart- why?

"Why?" is a major creator of hunger in people, having answers for everything is a turn off. Being right is over-rated! Leaving a question creates hunger and my heart sang again. I felt more saved than I had all day. And what's more I believe it, it's that kind of sowing I can do all day, every day. It's real to my life - it is life!

Mark Lowe

Living it out in the everyday is not new. St. David knew something about it. We don't know a lot about David. "Buchedd Dewi" - The life of David was written by Rhygyfarch of Llanbadarn Fawr some 500 years after David's death. Tradition states he was trained at St Illtud's school, also that he went on preaching missions with others such as Teilo, Cadog and Padarn. He was known as the 'waterman' because of the austere life he and his monks led although they extended generous hospitality to visitors, the old, the weak and the poor.

The last words of St. David are powerful - "Lords, brothers and sisters, rejoice and persevere in your faith and your belief, and do the little things that you have heard and seen in me".

It is the power of an ordinary life lived fully for Jesus. Gwenallt a prophetic poet voice in Wales captures something of this

"I saw David travelling from country to country like a gypsy of God
The Gospel and the Altar in his caravan;
…On the steelworks platform he put on his visor and the blue shirt
Showing the Christian rendered pure
Like metal in the furnace.
Put the sacred vessels on the kitchen table
And got bread from the pantry and rough wine from the cellar".

And in case we didn't get it the first time he wrote it another way - "David brought the church to our homes, and took bread from the pantry and bad wine from the cellar, and stood behind the table like a tramp so as not to hide the wonder of the sacrifice from us. After the communion we chatted by the fireside and he talked to us about God's natural order, the person, the family, the nation, and the society of nations, and the Cross keeping from turning any one of them into a god".[5]

> What I do you cannot do;
> but what you do, I cannot do.
> The needs are great, none of us
> including me ever do great things.
> But we can all do small things,
> with great love, and together
> we can do something wonderful."
> Mother Theresa of Calcutta [6]

NIGEL'S BLOG

In October 2002 the church buy me a year's membership for the Diplomat's Health Suite because I had no money and had just come back from Rehab. It is not always easy to be there, the manager and the cleaner are always playing with the Tarot cards and there is a lot of sexual immorality happening in the place. The next year the manager gives me a free one year membership and the Lord tells me, "I have placed you here as a lighthouse for my Kingdom." I get some of my Christian friends to pray for me. Early February 2004 an old school friend shows up with his 16 year old daughter who had a bad injury in her knee. She is a very good footballer. In boldness I prayed for her and said it would be better than ever in 6 months (she got picked to play for the Welsh National Squad in Portugal in September 2005).

In September 04 I see an old friend, Paul, in the gym, actually he is my oldest daughter's step-father. He was a British runner-up and 3 times Welsh Champion Body Builder. He fell into drug addiction, alcohol and splits with his wife - my ex-girlfriend. He says to me, "I want what you have got, you're beaming, you're glowing you are a lighthouse." He comes to see me at my workplace, Chooselife Drug and Alcohol Centre, which is part of Antioch. He has massive conviction of sin and asks the Bro into his life. More people are coming to Jesus, I am praying for more sick people and more Christians are coming to the gym. The Tarot card cleaner leaves and the new cleaner is a Christian. A lady, Diana, who is now part of Antioch becomes a Christian in the sauna. In October 05 am telling someone about the love and power of Jesus and an old friend butts in and starts joking around. He says, "Pray for me then," because they have been trying for a baby and she isn't catching. In December I am there again and fifteen stone of beef comes running towards me, grabs me lifts me up in the air and says to me, "Thanks mate!" I say, "Are you off your head," he says, "No I am going to be a dad, Praise the Lord!"

It is going good but there is still a Buddha on the wall in the Health Suite. So me being me I started praying for the Lord to split this Buddha in half. My friend Mike has been praying for the owner-manager to pull it down himself. The ceiling started to fall down. So myself, Paul and friends helped to put up a new ceiling. We have shown Rob the Dip (the manager) the caring love of Jesus being there when there is no-one else. After the ceiling was finished Rob and me was looking at the Pool Area. It was all bright and clean. Rob says to me, "Nigel it looks dark down at the end of the pool." (where the Buddha is). He asks me if the Buddha has got to come down. I say, "Your choice." - IT IS NO LONGER THERE - JESUS - HE RULES EVERYWHERE".

Nigel Haddock

GO DEEPER WALKING THE LAND

WHAT DOES IT MEAN TO BE "IN HIS FACE"?

Look with fresh eyes at God's commission and command to Adam in Genesis 1:27-28
"So God created man in His own image; in the image of God He created him; male and female He created them. Then God blessed them, and God said to them, "Be fruitful and multiply; fill the earth and subdue it; have dominion over the fish of the sea, over the birds of the air, and over every living thing that moves on the earth".

God creates the world then man in His image specifically to fill, subdue, and have dominion over it. This was what He wanted man and woman to do in the Garden, with the consequent fall, man's dominion over creation was lost. However God gave a promise of a seed who would come and restore this dominion.

It is integral to the whole of the New Testament that this is why Jesus, Son of God and Son of Man, came, and to reconcile the world to Himself. In Christ we are new creations, part of this new world order, but very much with the same purpose of filling the earth and, in New Testament terms, bringing in His Kingdom Rule and Authority. So in its simplest expression, walking the land is a going out to multiply and to call out for His Kingdom to come.

Then there's Abraham's story, of being led to that greater city. Each place he entered and dwelt he built an altar to worship and call on the Lord - with that promise of the seed in his heart. These uninhabited places later became the dwelling places of His seed.

By causing a servant to walk the land, the Lord would often be preparing a place for his coming purposes. Consider these examples:
- Joseph being sent before his brothers to Egypt.
- Moses flees Egypt, and prepares a way in the desert.
- Spies were sent into the promised land in order to give a good report.
- Jesus sent out his disciples to the places He intended to visit Himself, as he also did with the 70.
- The apostles missionary journeys opened up the way for the expansion of the kingdom, but often were preceded by those fleeing persecution.

Jesus walking the land

Jesus ministry was one of walking the land and bringing the kingdom to every situation. He then drew his disciples into this life: Mathew 9:35ff.

"Then Jesus went about all the cities and villages, teaching in their synagogues, preaching the gospel of the kingdom, and healing every sickness and every disease among the people. But when He saw the multitudes, He was moved with compassion for them, because they were weary and scattered, like sheep having no shepherd. Then He said to His disciples, 'The harvest truly is plentiful, but the labourers are few. Therefore pray the Lord of the harvest to send out labourers into His harvest'".

Mathew 10 then opens with the calling and appointing of the 12 apostles to do this very thing He had been doing. That is sending out labourers into the harvest fields.

So walking the land could be seen in these very terms - responding to Christ's compassion for the sheep without a shepherd and a going out to them in His authority.

Luke's version at this point records the sending of the 70 and states (10:1): "After these things the Lord appointed seventy others also, and sent them two by two before His face into every city and place where He Himself was about to go".

'before His face' - this is a literal translation, which is usually rendered 'before Him' or ahead of Him or similar. It is a reflection of the Hebrew word 'paniym' literally 'before face' but meaning presence. It also has a sense of 'in His face'. So that in a very real sense, to go before His face - ie to go ahead of where He is going is a going in His presence. - this will be reflected in 'carrying His presence').

Then the whole of Matthew 10 and Luke 10 is like a walk the land charter. Importantly in Mathew 10:40-42, there is an acknowledgement by the Anointed one of this dynamic, and affirmation of those who receive and warning against those who refuse such sent ones. "He who receives you receives Me, and he who receives Me receives Him who sent Me. He who receives a prophet in the name of a prophet shall receive a prophet's reward. And he who receives a righteous man in the name of a righteous man shall receive a righteous man's reward. And whoever gives one of these little ones only a cup of cold water in the name of a disciple, assuredly, I say to you, he shall by no means lose his reward".

Carrying His presence.

"After these things the Lord appointed seventy others also, and sent them two by two before His face into every city and place where He Himself was about to go" (Luke 10:1).

As we have seen this phrase 'before His face' is a literal translation, which on one level refers to Jesus' intention of also visiting these places. However it mirror's the Old Testament word for presence, which is a place of being before God's very face. Were Jesus an average man on the street, then we would understand Him as saying, 'You go ahead guys, I'll catch up with you.' However Jesus is no average man, He is God on earth, in the Flesh. So we have to understand what He is saying in this light. So though Jesus the man did not physically enter every town with them, in the most real sense possible, they carried His Presence with them. The proof of this is that the Kingdom of God came in power wherever they went, revealing the presence of the King within them.

In its simplest form a kingdom is where a king reigns and has dominion. When I believe and confess Jesus as Lord and Saviour then He becomes my king and sets up his throne, by the Spirit, in my heart. 1 Corinthians 3:16 (also 6:19), states that we are the very temple of God, and that the Spirit of God dwells in us.

So thinking along these lines, with the Spirit of God within me, wherever I go He is. I am carrying His presence, I am before His face continually.

This is a restoration of God's creation purpose for mankind. He made us in His image and likeness to bring in His dominion over the whole earth. For this to happen He formed Adam from the very earth and then put His breath as our life within us. God, Father, Son and Spirit in perfect unity opened up Their circle of relationship to include us. In Adam and Eve we lost this 'co-union' with God and were lost. In Jesus, by the Spirit, I find myself restored to this place of communion with God, so that in Him I can once again be fruitful and multiply, go out to fill and subdue the earth, bringing in His Kingdom reign. The confidence and authority for this comes from his presence within me.

Looking at the OT we see so many illustrations of this principle of carrying his presence:

Enoch walked with God until he was taken up (Genesis 5:24). "Then the Lord said to Noah, 'Come into the ark ... because I have seen that you are righteous before me in this generation'" Genesis 7:1, before Noah entered, God was present in the vessel used to save mankind.

The Lord gives a promise to Jacob at Bethel, that He will be with him and will keep him wherever he goes, "and will bring you back to this land; for I will not leave you until I have done what I have spoken to you" (Gen 28:15).

When God saved His people from captivity in Egypt, He did so by sending His presence before them, even in the literal sense of a fiery cloudy pillar. This is highlighted in one instance when Moses pleads with God not to withdraw His presence. Whilst Moses was up the mountain receiving revelation about making the Tabernacle, a dwelling place for God with man, the people were worshipping a man made idol, a golden calf. Turning away from his anger towards them, nevertheless, God now downgrades His promise of presence to, 'And I will send My Angel before you, and I will drive out the Canaanite and the Amorite and the Hittite and the Perizzite and the Hivite and the Jebusite. Go up to a land flowing with milk and honey; for I will not go up in your midst, lest I consume you on the way, for you are a stiff-necked people" (Exodus 33:2-3). No longer would God be with them, but His Angel. Moses, recognising the seriousness of this shift pleads with the Lord (33:12ff) "If Your presence does not go with us, do not bring us up from here. For how then will it be known that Your people and I have found grace in Your sight, except You go with us? So we shall be separate, Your people and I, from all the people who are upon the face of the earth". Unless His presence was in their midst, then they were no different from anyone else. Relenting, the Lord causes his goodness and glory to pass before Moses and speaks His name, "The LORD, the LORD God, merciful and gracious, long-suffering, and abounding in goodness and truth, keeping mercy for thousands, forgiving iniquity and transgression and sin, by no means clearing the guilty, visiting the iniquity of the fathers upon the children and the children's children to the third and the fourth generation" (Exodus 34:6-7). Instantly Moses falls on his face before God and pleads for His presence in their midst at which point God renews His covenant with them. He Himself will enter the land before them and drive out their enemies. Only they are to walk before Him in holiness keeping His covenant and commandments.

The fulfilment of this is seen in Joshua's conquest of the Promised land, the first stage of which is a symbolic act, the very ark of His Presence is carried before the people.

See also the various victories the people of God had when the Lord went up before them.

Turning to the New Testament, during Jesus' ministry we see in a limited sense that the disciples sent out in His name, carried His presence. The only limitation being that until Jesus ascended to His Father, the Spirit would not be released upon all flesh. He charges them to go into the whole world to multiply disciples soaked in the Father Son and Spirit, knowing that He is with them always (Matthew 28:18-20). Indications are given by Jesus as to what is to follow. For example in John 7:37-39, He declares that if we believe in Him, His very Spirit will flow out of our innermost being. This speaks not only of carrying His Presence but of being a springing well of His Presence. This of course is fulfilled at the outpouring of Presence at Pentecost. Being filled with the Spirit the Disciples pour out onto the street and the crowds gather to marvel. Peter explains in power that that which they are responding to is the very Presence of God by His Spirit.

In Acts 8 we see Philip repeating the pattern of Matthew 10. The counterfeit sorcery of Simon is shown up for what it is by the Presence in Philip. Acts 9:31 describes the churches 'walking in the fear of the Lord and in the comfort of the Holy Spirit and they were multiplied'. Acts 10 sees an outpouring of the Spirit even without Peter initiating anything, all that was required was for him to carry the Presence and speak the Good News. Time and again we read of the believers being, baptised and filled with the Spirit and so empowered to bring transformation.

Paul's letters emphasise the necessity of Christ in us, it is His presence in us that is the very hope of glory (Colossians 1:27). His prayer for the church in Ephesians 1:13-23 pours out the fullness of what carrying His Presence means. But here he takes it on to another level showing how the church as Christ's body is to be the fullness of Him who fills all things in every way. So there is a corporate carrying His Presence as well as individual, indeed we 'are being built together into a dwelling place of God in the Spirit' (Ephesians 2:22).

Hywel Rhys Edwards

CONNECT

In the light of the teaching in the GO DEEPER - WALKING THE LAND section meditate and reflect on Joshua 1:3, "I will give you every place where you set your foot."

What does it mean to you?

Just to remind us why we do this stuff -

"JUST TO SEE ME!" - Monkton, Pembrokeshire

   As a group we went to a council estate in Monkton, Pembrokeshire, split into pairs and wandered around. Apart from a mangy dog looking for trouble we didn't connect with anyone so walked on down a hill towards a gypsy camp. Two young boys tried to warn us off because of the violence and as we entered the site it felt unpredictable. I knocked on one of the caravan doors and a short old lady with only a few teeth left and an incontinence problem answered - her face the colour and grooves of a walnut. I explained that we were on the estate giving out free food bags simply to give people a reason to believe that God is good. She was amazed and exclaimed, " You mean that He sent you here JUST TO SEE ME!" I assured her that He had, and she invited us in to her caravan. We sat on her plastic covered sofa and spent some time with her. We were soon joined by a few young lads (I think they may have been the boys who warned us off) and a greyhound all interested in the visitors and being involved in deciding who to pass the food bags on to. As we left a police car was driving slowly on to the site.

Deb Chapman

The Holy Spirit is the Spirit of Jesus and as we walk we carry His presence and as He goes with us we are given the possibility of both adventuring with Him and of resting in Him as we seek to do the things we see the Father doing. His Spirit, His presence provokes reaction. He is not tame, He is grace in technicolour, demands response or woos it, comes as a raging fire or as a gentle touch. He wants to be asked to walk with us - not messed with.

JOURNEY TO THE MARGINS

JOURNEY TO THE MARGINS

At the end of a few uncomfortable days of travelling in a rough vehicle, of frustrating misses in connecting with people and the niggles of a worn-down team, it all seemed a waste of time. Yet the last person I spoke to that day, after, a thrown together B-B-Q on a nowhere estate was called Pearl. The B-B-Q itself became a bizarre kingdom of heaven party.

Three generations from one family come to the B-B-Q on the estate where no one wants to live- "Twenty years we've been here, five sisters all live over there, one with eight children [she can't cope] my daughter and two grandchildren".

We get invited into homes as we invite people to come. Some lads, drunk, go looking for their friends, to invite them, they are addicts and a number have been in prison. They are amazed we are doing this for them out of our own money. In a few gaps in the flow of obscenities, anger mixed with laughter, they talk about their lives. One admits that he went to church when he was in prison. Some of the women ask whether we can start something in their homes. It is the first place where I have been hugged and kissed twice simply for being there.

We pray for a word of knowledge and, get one, so that we can invite a little boy who we have seen wandering around for the last day and night. We knock on a door, the right one, and find that Kane lives there with his mum and her sixteen year old partner. Kane, a restless three or four year old, has been playing alone all day, appearing on different parts of the site

solemn and wary. Marked with the blood money of drugs and the violence of neglect. Self sufficient, throwing stones, a good aim, and breaking things that don't matter, no trouble, wants his Mum, and wants not to be left, but knows it is dangerous to be seen or to demand. Kane wary with rejection and tired wants to come to the B-B-Q.

Pearl was too fearful to come over, she was fairly new to the site, nervous of the addicts, disabled, with four children, she wants us to come back and visit her in her home so we can talk more. Her name is a reminder that I have become rich. Jesus, the pearl of great price gave it all away to buy a people and a patch of earth. This makes us also the treasure he risked the loss of everything to gain. For me that makes a difference; it means that we join Him in a reckless treasure hunt.

In Wales, the wealth has been mined and quarried out years ago, but you still see the colour in the land, Nantlle slate an unexpected grey and pink, in roofs and steps. There is treasure too in the lives sucked dry on heroin but what do we see? Jesus asked His disciples, "Who do you say I am?" The standard answers, the popular opinions, didn't cut it - the revelation answer to this question defined Peter and defines us. The "Who do you say I am " question is there in a different way in everyone we meet. We need the revelation of the living God to see the answer behind the person.

"No-one wants to be a drug addict or alcoholic, but this doesn't stop people from becoming addicted. The most commonly asked question is simply - how? How could my son, daughter, father, sister, or brother become a liar, a thief, someone who could not be trusted? How could this happen? And why won't they stop? Alcohol and addictive drugs are basically painkillers. They chemically kill physical or emotional pain. They make people numb. For drugs to be attractive to a person, there must first be some underlying unhappiness, sense of hopelessness, or physical pain that they want to escape."[1]

ALAN AND RACHEL INTERVIEW

Alan : "I started off in crime at a very young age. I was abused physically and sexually and I became another person full of rejection and rebellion. I let the circumstances of my past dictate the direction of my future. For some reason I thought that when I reached a certain age I would stop. But what I found was that after being in Detention Centre, Care, Borstal, I couldn't just stop, the system had become a way of life.

I got into drugs at the late age of 20 because at that time they weren't easily available - unlike now. I became like a vampire willing to do anything to get hold of drugs. I was in prison every year for fifteen years. Addicted to drugs I broke into chemists and committed armed robberies to feed my addiction. I used to look at older cons and think that would be me as I couldn't see a way out. I got out of prison full of good intentions only to find myself back in again. I escaped from prison when I only had six weeks left to serve and ended up in Dartmooor.

I was so desperate that I didn't care how I changed I just wanted to change. Some friends had become Christians and one day in a prison cell I called out to Jesus to help me and He did. It hasn't been easy but fourteen years later I am still following Jesus. When I walk through the town addicts I know look at me with their defenses down thinking, "He's still there." I am married with children and work as the Director of Chooselife Drug and Alcohol Intervention Service. We want to love people and be there for them. Jesus is a friend of sinners, loved sinners. We don't want to love people just because we want to see them saved. We want to see them saved because we love them, but we will keep loving them regardless... Justin "Crim," twenty year old heroin addict in prison, given up on life goes into Christian Rehab, two years later he has become a Christian, he is re-united with his family and is looking forward to the future.

We have lost close friends to overdoses, people who you could see had real destiny on their lives. One of my closest friends was touched by God in a powerful way - he lived off it for three days and then decided to go back on to drugs. Everytime I saw him we talked about Jesus, but there was no change until one day I said he would have no peace until he came back to Him ,,, he is now doing life in prison for a manslaughter he didn't commit - his family is totally wrecked. But he is now searching again for God.

`Sometimes it means talking to ministers in the Welsh Assembly - I'm scared, praying, "Why have you put me here?" Me doing training for Magistrates, finding favour in the Courts, negotiating rehab with Pprosecutors who used to lock me up. What a turn around! Friendship with a Clerk of the Court who nearly gave up on their first day on the job after seeing me yelling abuse at all the Magistrates. It's mad! It is all His grace and that is what I keep hanging onto. The thief came to steal, kill and destroy. Jesus came to give life and that's what He keeps giving me and many others."

Known

I could name them,
Maybe not their given names
but their known names.
They didn't die in trenches
but in bedsits drunk on sick.
Death by prescription.
Focused lads, focused on
the next hit, the means to get it,
pain finds a way
to die alone in a cell
or with friends on a chair in a room
where others have died.
Funerals with a difference
partners exchanged like needles
drugs dealt at the graveside
and still the waterfall of grief
wet air to eat, dark mist
the falls grey shadow,
a journey down
wrapped in fragile strength
of rainbows.

Rachel : "I ran a prison Family Centre in England, I am now married to Alan and run the Family Centre in Chooselife. It is hard for the families of those with addictions. We want them to know that they are worth something. It means being consistent, taking a little girl to visit her mum in prison for 6 years so that they can still have a relationship. It means seeing children locked in their own world, full of sadness, learning to play knowing that they are special. It means parenting classes, parents who have never played themselves learning to play with their children, starting to see their own childhood restored. It means being there giving a sense of family, a sense of belonging, encouragement, support and praise. The trips out, the visits to the homes matter but the small things that show the kindness of Jesus matter more, even when we don't always get it right."

"The gospel through the eyes of the poor is like a second conversion.
I was born again, again"[2]

CONNECT - PARTY TIME

" The next time you put on a dinner, don't just invite your friends and family and rich neighbours, the kind of people who will return the favour. Invite some people who never get invited out the misfits, from the wrong side of the tracks. You'll be- and experience- a blessing. They won't be able to return the favor, but the favor will be returned - oh how it will be returned at the resurrection of Gods people".

Ask Jesus what you should do and who you should invite.

POVERTY DEFINED

EXTREME POVERTY - households cannot meet basic needs for survival. They are chronically hungry, unable to access health care, lack the basic amenities of safe drinking water and sanitation, cannot afford education for some or all of the children, and perhaps lack rudimentary shelter- a roof to keep the rain out of the hut, a chimney to remove the smoke from the cook stove- and basic articles of clothing such as shoes. Unlike moderate and relative poverty, extreme poverty only occurs in developing countries.

MODERATE POVERTY- refers to conditions of life in which basic needs are met but just barely.

RELATIVE POVERTY - is generally construed as a household income level below a given proportion of average national income. The relatively poor, in high income countries, lack access to cultural goods , entertainment, recreation , and to quality healthcare, education and other prerequisites for upward social mobility". [3]

Matthew 25: 34 "Then the King will say to those on His right,' Come, you who are blessed by my Father; take your inheritance, the kingdom prepared for you since the creation of the world. For I was hungry and you gave me something to eat, I was thirsty and you gave me something to drink, I was a stranger and you invited me in, I needed clothes and you clothed me, I was sick and you looked after me, I was in prison and you came to visit me. Then the righteous will answer him, 'Lord, when did we see you hungry and feed you, or thirsty and give you something to drink? When did we see you a stranger and invite you in ,or needing clothes and clothe you? When did we see you sick or in prison and go to visit you?' The King will reply , ' I tell you the truth, whatever you did for one of the least of these brothers of mine you did it for me.' "

I still find it painful to read this passage, yet there was a time when I could barely read it at all because the challenge of it was so far removed from the life I was living, even though I was "in Mission" at the time. The priority of the poor changed and is changing the focus of my life.

There is an imperative to feed and clothe the poor, the love of Jesus compels it yet it becomes much more than food and clothes it can became a connection with his love , with his compassion - for all involved.

Reflect on personal priorities and choices in the light of this scripture.

The Celtic Christians understood the imperative of the gospel for the poor. They deliberately focused on the most needy. They also challenged the injustice and structural sin of the day and through the conversion of kings and tribal chiefs structures and society were changed. The "Senches Mor", the record of the Laws of Ireland state; "Retaliation prevailed in Ireland before Patrick, and Patrick brought forgiveness with him. So now, no one is executed for his crimes as long as he pays 'evic' - the blood fine".[5] Patrick also confronted slavery, he had experienced it first hand.

The poor are not a project amongst many demands and cries they are THE CRY: the children orphaned in war, through aids and famine, the child soldiers, slaves and sex workers- the women alongside the children, the poorest of the poor.

I have seen the desperation of Tsunami victims, held children and babies with AIDS, touched the hopelessness of the sick and hungry , the dead eyes of children and teenagers involved in the sex trade. This has

When the history of our time is written, there will probably be three things that come out of it - the internet, this war against terror, and the fact that an entire continent burst into flames while we all stood around with watering cans.
You cannot ignore the AIDS emergency".
BONO.[4]

changed my priorities - it is supposed to. It has also changed my priorities in the nation in which I live where poverty, in world terms, is barely poverty but leaves the same stains of shame, worthlessness, hopelessness and fear. It wears the clothes of addiction, of abuse, the wear down of violence, poor housing and of debt.

WORTH IT?

Luke 9:57,58 "A man said to him 'Lord I will follow you wherever you go' and Jesus said to him 'Foxes have holes and birds of the air have nests, but the Son of Man has nowhere to lay his head'".

Jesus was full of purpose, He set His face towards Jerusalem, towards His death. The journey was one of incredible vulnerability, vulnerability a choice He made. He chose to get up wet with dew and aching from cold earth. Heaven was His home, a place to lay His head where creation stretched about Him, stars and celestial beings as dimensions He could fully own and walk amongst.

Yet He chose to live as a dependent tramp, dependent on the hospitality of others, dependant on the gifts of money from the women who followed Him. In Bethany He had the closest thing to home in the house of Lazarus, Mary and Martha. He was a friend of sinners, He chose to make his home with the outcasts, the rejects - those of despised profession, morality and status, sinners and the sick. No wonder He fell asleep in the boat before the waves of human need could hit with the shoreline - He was exhausted.

Today there is still the wear down factor of not knowing where you will sleep at night or if you will eat. There is the responsibility you have for others with you, the sheer discomfort of sleeping rough in the dirt and the rain. The not-quite-sound sleep because of the vulnerability to weather and to violence ... This absolutely nothing as relentless as for those who have no choice - the refugees, the street sleepers in the cities, the totally destitute in the gutters of India. Those who sleep in the day as feet walk over them, naked babies and children utterly vulnerable in a deadness of sleep yet finding it safer to sleep in the day than risk it by night.

So why sleep rough, until there is an invite to a home? It is in part the rhythm of the desert, the drawing aside to pray in wilderness, or as much as can be found in our industrialised West. It is a

> "IT WON'T DO FOR PEOPLE WHO ARE SET TO LEAD A REVOLUTION TO BE THIN-SKINNED'
> Catherine Booth[6]

> "The Son of Man came eating and drinking, and they say, 'Here is a glutton and a drunkard, a friend of tax collectors and 'sinners'. But wisdom is proved right by her actions."
> Matthew 11:19

desire to identify with those who have no choice - a relief of shallow identification in a slept out prayer. It is also the adventure and privilege, albeit with sleeping bags and bivvy bags, of laying a head on the chest of Him who had no place to lay His head. It is the sheer absurdity of dragging yourself out of a hedge and into a café for an all day breakfast and scrapping off the dirt before another day of wandering, hopefully, with His presence.

And there is still the same call to go wherever, to do whatever He asks - no safety nets except relationship with Him and others. The initial excitement of not knowing where to go, what to do soon wears off and becomes the greater confidence that He knows and that whatever it looks like it is o.k. The joy of walking free, of going to the limits that He sets, of following Him into a new day is good. It is the way He wasted his time with the poor and powerless, pouring His life away in prayer with His father, praying for the sick, teaching the crowds, eating in a home, walking establishing the kingdom in power and in proclamation - really good.

We are called to deliberately seek out the poor. If we go to the poor maybe others will be raised up, a mobilised mix of mercy and direct encounter, amongst the loneliness and pain of those who have no framework, maybe no way to survive .

Sometimes bizarre things happen that unwittingly draw you into involvement. In Ireland on the way to catch a ferry, we came across a cat that had been run over and left on the roundabout of a small town. The cat had a broken back and half a jaw missing. We carried it to a vet along the street, to be met by an obviously mad, elderly, one-eyed receptionist. She didn't know the cat and barely seemed to know the vet who, understandably, didn't call much. She suggested we put the cat down, although she explained it was against the law.

Found myself in a dingy back room with a few jars of odd-looking potions and a needle. My friends bravely held the cat down - whilst

> 'OWN ONLY WHAT YOU CAN ALWAYS CARRY WITH YOU; KNOW LANGUAGES KNOW COUNTRIES,KNOW PEOPLE. LET YOUR MEMORY BE YOUR TRAVEL BAG"
> Solzynhytsyn[7]

HISTORY ST CUTHBERT

Moreover, he was wont to resort most commonly unto those places and preach in those hamlets lying afar off in steep and craggy hills, which other men had dread to visit , and which from their poverty as well as uplandish rudeness teachers shunned to approach. And yet he did so gladly give himself to godly travail, and laboured so diligently in careful teaching of them, that he would go out of the monastery and oftentimes not come home again in an whole week, sometimes not in two or three, at times not even in a full month; but tarrying in the hilly parts, he would call the poor folk of the country to heavenly things with the word of preaching as well as work of virtuous example." [8]

trying not to be put down themselves - eventually the poor cat did succumb. The receptionist refused to dispose of the body - we ended up posting it into a litter bin - well what would you have done?!

A few days later I see a run-over dog in the road, obviously in terrible pain, there is an elderly man with the dog, the man seems confused and in shock though shouting that it is not his dog. Everyone is sitting in their cars watching, I have 'cat flashbacks', groan, get out of the car and suddenly everyone springs into action, they know the dog, they know the owner, they know the man - I get back in the car and drive off, thinking what was that all about?.

Without being over spiritual I felt like I was supposed to see something in this - apart from the obvious about avoiding cats and dogs with a death wish!

Maybe it is that sometimes we have to get involved even beyond our willingness and ability, sometimes our involvement will provoke those who really understand the situation to act. This is particularly the case if we want to make our priorities Biblical priorities "Others" - the poorest of the poor.

PRIORITY "OTHERS" - THE POOREST OF THE POOR

It is time to get involved with the poorest of the poor - the orphaned, the needy, the alien, the widowed. This is not an added extra, this is the heart of the gospel.

"He defended the cause of the poor and the needy, and so all
went well. Is that not what it means to know me." Jer 22:16

Jesus answered, "If you want to be perfect, go sell your possessions and give
to the poor, and you will have treasure in Heaven. Then come, follow me." Matt 19:21

"All they asked was that we should continue to remember the poor,
the very thing I was eager to do." Gal 2:10

"Others" William Booth's one word message by telegram early in the 1900's
to encourage his officers around the world."[9]

The poorest, the most broken world-wide are children and women, many living in the 10/40 window, "1.3 billion people with little chance to hear the gospel. Fully 85 percent of the world's poorest countries are here, and 40 percent of those populations are children. Tragically only 1.2 percent of Christian mission dollars go there". We can be overwhelmed by the need and the statistics. The statistics concerning the poorest of the poor are so extreme that they can numb us. Yet, we can do something to see the lives of individuals, communities, nations, transformed. "I was hungry and you gave me something to eat; I was thirsty and you gave me drink...I was naked and you clothed me".[13]

THe small steps, the small decisions we take, can change things whether it is sponsoring a totally destitute child or connecting with an orphanage or engaging in advocacy and action in the many different spheres.

Sometimes it takes many small steps and a focused determination to engage in making a difference in the ways you might long too. Don't give up - for their sake.

There are children worldwide living in economic slavery, street children, those involved in the sex trade and millions dying of hunger, preventable diseases and of course AIDS.

When I first saw the photograph I didn't believe it. I saw a row of toddlers, girls tied to chairs above an open drain. There were holes cut into the seats of the chairs. One child had tipped the chair over - often when this happens they are left to die in their own excrement - a scene from one of the many orphanages in China. Girl children, or children who are sick or disabled, are often killed at birth. The "one child policy" makes a boy very precious and a less than perfect child unwanted. If they escape death at birth they are often placed in orphanages to die, barely fed, unloved, untreated in sickness.

China... Yet the cry of the children is heard worldwide. Friends working in Sri Lanka were offered a boy of two for sex. The boy was offered to them by his brother for a handful of sweets. Under the age of eight, sex with a child can be bought for a few sweets, after that age you might pay, maybe a few dollars. Age and family are often no protection.

In Uganda a friend was walking in the bush and came across a group of children abandoned in a hut. Originally there had been a mother, father and 7 children. The father and two of the children had died of AIDS. Then, in the same year, the mother's brother and sister-in-law had died, so the mother had their five children to take care of as well. The ten children said they last saw their mum walking down a track into the bush, hands in the air and crying, "God how do you expect me to cope". They hadn't seen her again.

The children were emotionally devastated and malnourished. Initially, there was little the over-stretched group working into this part of Uganda could do for them. The cry of the children goes up, they are the ones most vulnerable to poverty, exploitation, war, famine and epidemics. "The poor will be with you always" (Matthew 26:11). That statement can lead to faith or fatalism, the cry of the children sounding worldwide can seem too immense an issue to handle.

In Brazil the altar of sacrifices often the same as ours, one of indifference or compromise. The plight of the street children is an uncomfortable irritant, something to be ignored by many Christians. A hard week at work, Saturday spent at home with the family, Sunday in church means that it can be inconvenient to care; although some do.

"I killed you because you had no future, no education and you were a nuisance" read the note around the neck of a nine year old boy murdered on the street. Jesus gave His life for that boy, His view would be rather diferent. In one Brazilian city, friends of ours were shocked to see a group of Satanists doing a soup run for the kids. What was their motive?

Millions of street kids translate into individuals like Daniel and his brother, boys of six and seven. Sniffing glue to numb their pain, they had vague memories of a mother, and didn't know how long they had been on the streets. Their desire, "A mum and dad and a computer game". Our eldest son, age four at the time, was deeply impacted by these two throwaway children. Many are caught in a spiral of sin and violence, trapped in prostitution, drug and solvent abuse. Destroyed by the supposed freedom of the streets. Jesus is the only one who can break this sickening cycle.

Sometimes we ease the pain by saying that these people, these children, these parents don't feel as we do, they don't care as we would. I saw the pain of a Kurdish mother who saw her 2 children die in the mountain winter as she escaped persecution. Her children at that time were the same age as mine, was her pain any less than mine would be? Her grief for her child of two and a half and a baby of six months was completely overwhelming. The question for us all in these situations is, do we operate in fatalism or faith? Fatalism says give up - nothing can change, what difference can one person make. What difference can one church make, what difference can a group of churches working together make?

Yet faith can make a way. Faith can shake a nation. Christians with the justice and zeal of God in their hearts have changed situations so complex, so immersed in sin it seemed impossible. At times the word of God is so challenging it hurts and tears us to read it. It has power to ease us out of being comfortable. It forces us to take risks.

Information and exposure to situations also changes us. In the Britain of the Second World War, hundreds of thousands of children were evacuated from cities that were being bombed. Middle and upper class families realised for the first time the deplorable conditions in the nation's industrial cities. A new social concern was born.

"Some of the children were crawling with lice and never used a toilet, they simply relieved themselves anywhere in the house. Some had never slept in a bed, one boy said he never went to sleep lying down".

In the evacuation hosts could often chose the children they would look after in their homes, "... the pretty and attractive ones went first and I thought I would never belong, one little girl was in tears because no-one would have her and she came to me and said, 'Doesn't anyone want me?'"[10]

As we open our eyes to God's word a radical life-style may affect our families. God puts "the lonely in families". It won't simply be a concern for the lost at a distance. It will also be the lost on our doorstep. Yet, religious people often find ministry to children a distraction, second class, not really the task of the gospel. Amy Carmichael, the missionary from Dohnavur in India said of her work rescuing child prostitutes, "Could it be right to turn from so much, that might be of profit, and become just nursemaids?"[11] The answer to her life and ministry was a resounding "Yes", which challenged both India and the world.

Today the work of Rolland and Heidi Baker,[12] started amongst orphans and the children on the rubbish dumps of Mozambique, is a revival which is challenging the world.

SARAH'S STORY - DON'T GIVE UP

Even when you know what you want to do it can be a torturous route to get there. Sarah became a Christian in university and felt that God was leading her to work with the poor, probably in the slums. She left university without debt and with very few possessions. She decided to do 'a year out' discipleship training course. Over the next years amongst other things she managed a community business, worked in inner city Atlanta amongst the homeless, herself living in a virtually derelict building, ran a programme there for men coming out of addiction, supported others as they built community in Costa Rica amongst the poor. Each of these things was good but she knew it wasn't what she was born for.

Then on her thirtieth birthday she found herself working in the slums of Delhi - she enjoyed the work, her administrative gift was put to good use but again it wasn't "it". In each of these situations she learnt a lot and as someone who is faithful and hard working gave a lot. There were also the times in between things, problems with visas etc when she felt she was just hanging around wasting her life.

She is now pioneering, with a friend in Delhi, a home where teenage girls who have come out of the sex trade will be able to find freedom and healing in a family environment. At the moment of writing they have four girls and a new baby with them (two of the girls are HIV +), they can take six. In the end they want to see a network of homes develop where some of the girls could then go and help and support other girls in similar situations. There are hardly any other organisations working in this particular way where they are.

What have the girls come out of? In the main red light area in Delhi most of the windows of the brothels have bars on them so the women peer out with a look of complete hopelessness and sadness caged up behind the bars. At the current rate of growth by 2025 one in five Indian girl children will be a prostitute.

The factors causing women and girls to enter into prostitution are numerous but mostly stem from poverty. Girls (as young as seven) are sold by poor parents, tricked into fraudulent marriages, or promised employment only to find themselves in Indian brothels. Many entering against their will are locked up for days, starved, beaten and burned with cigarettes and electric wires until they learn how to service up to twenty-five clients a day. Some girls go through training which can include constant exposure to pornographic films and being repeatedly raped. It can take a girl sold into this debt-bondage fifteen years to purchase her freedom".

Sarah and Louise have called the home "Atulya" which in Hindi means without price; unequalled, immeasurable, unique.

Sarah thinks this has been worth the wait.

BULGARIA ORPHANAGE

The Bulgarian Christians had been visiting the state run orphanage for about 3 years when I took my second group of women from Wales into the home to do creative workshops. Being very poor, the Bulgarians had been able to give very little material help, but Pastor Yavor knew each child and had consistently shown and shared with them the love of their heavenly Father.

As Yavor led the youngsters in worship, the heavy presence of the Holy Spirit settled on the bare, draughty room. The hard faces of the teenagers softened, the desperation and pain becoming visible. The faces of the smaller children, dressed in odd assortments of donated clothes, lit up.

Alison from Wales stepped forward to give her testimony through the translator. She told them how she too had been unwanted, abandoned in a children's home by her mother. She gently shared the catalogue of abuse and rejection she had suffered, until she ended up a heroin addict begging on a blanket on the street.

Many of the older teens instantly connected with her story. With no family or state help once they left the home, they faced the grim possibility of unemployment and homelessness. A life of crime on the streets stared them in the face. Several of the girls were already known to be involved in prostitution.

Alison finished her story by simply sharing how Jesus changed her life as she asked Him to be her friend. As Yavor gave the appeal the response to Jesus was overwhelming and from the heart.

What struck me was that most Bulgarian children never have the opportunity to hear the gospel. What's more, from my experience of the country, it's often a struggle to really break through into the presence of God in worship. Yet here was God pouring out His tangible presence and grace on the poorest and the least. God was eager to meet with abandoned and desperate children.

We want to work with the Bulgarian church to help set up a home for those leaving the orphanage as they transition into adult life. Maybe the future for Bulgaria will be built by orphans transformed by the Father's love.

Elizabeth Watkins

CONNECT - PRAY THE BIBLE

Pray these Scriptures as a Prayer.

MERCY
Father in Heaven, You have said:
He who oppresses the poor shows contempt for their Maker,
but whoever is kind to the needy honours God.
Rich and poor have this in common:
The Lord is the Maker of them all.
So I will not exploit the poor because they are poor
nor crush the needy in court, for You will take up their case
and will plunder those who plunder them.
The righteous care about justice for the poor,
but the wicked have no such concern.
And You say, he who is kind to the poor lends to the Lord,
and He will reward him for what he has done.
Let me be like Job who said:
I rescued the poor who cried for help,
and the fatherless who had none to assist him.
The man who was dying blessed me;
I made the widow's heart sing.
I was eyes to the blind and feet to the lame.
I was a father to the needy; I took up the case of the stranger.
I broke the fangs of the wicked
And snatched the victims from their teeth.

Proverbs 14:31; 22:2,22-23; 29:7; 19:17; Job 29:12-13, 15-17, 25)

Then ask Him to show you His heart for the least, for the children.

Ask Him what He would like you to do, what steps He would like you to take.

Tell someone about these steps and take them, that dreams and visions might become reality.[13]

YOUNG PEOPLE TO THE NATIONS

Young people are full of good will to those less well off than themselves. For the past couple of years our youth club has visited two orphanages in Bulgaria to spend time with the residents. In order to come our young people, aged from nine to nineteen, have to raise several hundred pounds for their own expenses and money to provide activities in the orphanages.

Their creativity in fund-raising is inspiring to watch. They make biscuits, wash cars, baby-sit, clean houses, hold boot sales, save pocket money, do sponsored silences and bike rides, open their own beauty salons and fill penny jars. All of this so they can spend the week serving others.

The fund-raising activities are building blocks in the friendship of the team. We work together in various groupings for the few months before the trip and get to know each other better. Working together for a common goal is a very uniting exercise. In the few weeks before we do workshops on Bulgarian culture and language. This means we can communicate on a very basic level. The Bulgarian church we work alongside provide translators but we find it really creates a keen response when we speak Bulgarian. The programme of activities varies each year, reflecting the gifting of the team. We do music, storytelling, puppetry, art, craft and lots of sport. We love spending time with the children and the activities are just a way of getting alongside them. There is always lots of laughter.

The children there have very little materially. In one of the orphanages a bar of soap to wash all the children has to last a week. When we talk to them about how much Jesus loves them and wants to know them the reaction is disbelief at first. They struggle to see their value because their life is so hard and they are treated by society as worth very little. In the kingdom of God they are truly precious and it is an incredible privilege to tell them that.

We try to help practically by improving their environment. Painting murals and providing instruments to be used there have left a lasting effect. They do so much with so little. Last year we left a keyboard with them. They recorded a four track CD with it and have had one of the tracks played on Bulgarian radio!

The rewards for us are immense. The young people we take develop in so many ways.

They literally have their hearts and minds expanded. They see their world differently and often they develop a deep appreciation of things they previously took for granted.

Some are going to visit for the third year. They have made friends with Bulgarian young people and want to continue to share their lives with them.

Ann O'Hare

At times in history there has been the systematic destruction of a generation of children. At the time of Moses an edict went out from Pharoah demanding the destruction of the Hebrew children. The life of Moses was spared - he was raised up as the one who would be a deliverer and lead the people of Israel out of Egypt.

At the time of Jesus, Herod tried to destroy the threat to his rule with the destruction of all male children of two and under. Jesus the Saviour was hidden in Egypt and God's purpose prevailed. Satan hates the children, he wants to see their lives snuffed out or perverted. There is a rising tide of destruction against children and young people worldwide. Could it be that the enemy is attempting to destroy the generation that will see the King return. Before the return of Jesus a significant prophecy is to be fulfilled, "Behold I will send you Elijah the prophet, before the coming of the great and terrible day of the Lord and he will turn the hearts of the fathers to the children, and the hearts of the children to the fathers, lest I come and strike the land with a curse" (Malachi 4:5-6).

We have a part to play in releasing children and young people to their inheritance in God. Even at this time, in the present move of the Holy Spirit, children and young people are being touched with a hunger and thirst for God. we need to consider how we release and equip them.

The expression of mission that they find may well be one that is unfamiliar to us or even makes us feel profoundly uncomfortable. We need to make sure, however, that in a subtle way, we are not helping 'Herod' and hindering God's purpose. Some of the most dynamic teams we send might be so young they frighten us. Young people who, in some situations have not been trusted with a small group, have ended up pioneering works amongst unreached people groups. A friend of ours, a young man in his twenties, going blind with a progressive eye disease has been able to birth a group of believers in one of the most unreached countries of the world. He has also established innovative business and relief projects. Our equipping needs to take serious account of this Joel's Army, they have a fighting chance of taking the land.

This also needs to be a consideration in our resourcing and training partnerships in other nations. Each will have their own Joel's Army whose stream will fill out the river of God's purpose.

JOURNEY TO HIDDEN PEOPLES,
OTHER NATIONS

JOURNEY TO HIDDEN PEOPLES, OTHER NATIONS

The greatest poverty is to be lost. Jesus came, a friend of sinners to seek and save the lost He is not willing that any should perish, but maybe we are. There is little focus, in real terms, on those who have never had the opportunity to hear the gospel and to experience the kingdom. At times it seems impossible to make a difference but we can, if we want to enough. New, emerging, mission movements from the developing world are leading the way - which is great. They want to enough, and will sacrifice for the privilege. And it is a privilege.

Hidden peoples of other nations, people groups despised within their own cultures, form a subversive map illuminating the world with hidden colour. Often these peoples have never had an opportunity to come to faith in Jesus. There is often no indigenous church and the oppressive religious and political systems they live under make it illegal see such a church emerge. These people matter - they are mostly as poor physically as they are spiritually. We are the inheritors by faith of the promise made to Abraham and if all the 'families of the earth' are to be blessed through us they have to be our priority.

We can only invest our lives, our prayers, our resources in a certain number of directions. In a very cLear way we need to get in position for all that God wants to do. Let's be strategic in focus rather than flabby or sentimental. Often the spoken or unspoken vision statements of our lives reflect the parochial rather than the global. Jesus' vision statement was rather different, "But you shall recieve power, when the Holy Spirit has come upon you; and you shall be witnesses to me in Jerusalem and in all Judea and Samaria and to the ends of the Earth" (Acts 1:8).

Strategy points us to the 10/40 window, ministries amongst children and young people, the training and resourcing of nationals, and the 40/70 window which includes Europe, the nations on the Old Silk Road through Central Asia into China, the North of Korea and Japan.

The "Go" of Jesus draws us - "Then Jesus came to them and said, 'All authority in heaven and on earth has been given to me. Therefore go and

GO DEEPER - STRATEGY

ARE WE WISE OR FOOLISH?

In a deeper way we need to understand something of our redemptive purpose as nations but also the redemptive purpose in the movements of people and resources happening worldwide. Two hundred years ago the coastlands of the world were the target. William Carey was an initial pioneer of this in India. A century or so ago Hudson Taylor founded the China Inland Mission and attention was focused on the interior of continents. In the twentieth century the cry of the unreached people groups has been heard. The inspiring work of William Cameron Townsend and the Wycliffe Bible Translators led the way.

Over the last decade of the twentieth century there was a growing focus on the 10/40 window where eighty percent of the unreached world now lives, many of them in "gateway cities." In this area the poorest people in the world live, the ones with the lowest life expectancy, the highest infant mortality rate and the highest illiteracy levels. Most of the world's totally unreached people groups live in this area. Spiritually it is the stronghold of Islam, Hinduism and Buddhism.

I wonder what it would be like if we asked a non-Christian businessman to assess how the Church of Christ is doing in the world at this time. In Luke 16:8 we read, " the sons of this world are more shrewd in their generation than the sons of light." Is this true of our approach to world evangelism? A valid question would be, "What is our long term goal or business plan". The answer might well be - the return of Jesus. Our strategy, world evangelisation. In Matthew 24 Jesus states that the gospel will be preached in every nation and then the end will come. The signs of the end of the age will be pestilence, famine, national disasters, wars and rumours of wars. nation, "ethnos" in the Greek is the root word for ethnic group, meaning that people from every ethnic group will be represented at the return of Jesus.

We would be asked about our resources. We could point to a world map and show the progress of the gospel over the last years, the church-rich and revival areas of the world. We would also speak of those in the resistant block. The question we might find embarrassing to answer is this -

"How much of the Church's resources world-wide in people and in finance go into the 10/40 window?" Our answer is about six percent at the most. On a business level it would be fair to question our integrity in the task. Our goal is perhaps merely an ideal. Could it be we're simply playing games?

GO DEEPER - GO CROSS-CULTURAL

Culture includes our behaviour, what we do. It involves our values, the things which are important to us. It involves beliefs, and what is true for us. It shapes our fundamental world view and answers we give to such questions as "Who are we?", "Why are we here?" To understand another culture it is often important to understand our own and our cultural blindspots. We also have to look at Jesus. We see the Son of God who gave up heaven, gave up the right to His life and entered a world of sin and pain which was so culturally alien that it was the ultimate cross-cultural expression of God's love. We also see how Jesus came as a man, in the form of a man, to fully identify with man. The ultimate identification was in dying for man and, on behalf of man, for man's sin.

We look at the way Jesus behaved. He behaved with humility. He did not impose, rather He drew people. He brought grace which fulfilled and overcame he law. As Jesus walked from place to place He saw things as they really were - no filters, no sunglasses, a sensitive heart and sensitive eyes. That which we have seen on television becomes a reality as we touch, smell, see. It can cut through the self protection which is a kind of slow death.

Jesus has been described as "God with skin on". Often when we pray for those who don't know Jesus we can be very detached. The answer isn't normally a nice prayer, but rather a person, someone with "skin on," a person with God in them. Someone who can tell and live what they have seen and heard and touched. When you cross a culture, you become a child. You don't understand what is going on. You don't know the language. Your attempts to speak it sound foolish. The resource of years is trapped behind the language of a toddler, "Please, food, me!" No-one knows that you are intelligent, sensitive or wise because you can't reveal the extent of your knowledge or understanding! You are experiencing culture shock. The depth to which you experience it depends on many factors of background and personality. Symptoms of culture shock can be minor sickness,

depression, intense loneliness, anxiety, low self-esteem and feelings of failure. All the external props and securities have been taken away. Yet to succeed, culture shock has to be worked through. There needs to be an immediate bonding and identifying with the new culture. It is important that this happens within the first few weeks when we might long for things to be safe and comfortable - especially for the people we have 'sent' - we musn't rescue them from the process.

make disciples of all nations, baptising them in the name of the Father and of the Son and of the Holy Spirit, and teaching them to obey everything I commanded you. And surely I am with you always, to the very end of the Age'" (Matt 28:18-20).

The Greek word for "Go therefore" is "poreuthentes" which means "to depart, to leave, to cross boundaries"[14]. It is necessary to cross boundaries of race, culture, geography if we are to see people come to a fullness of life in Jesus. These sorts of boundaries can be profoundly uncomfortable and disorientating to cross but surely worth it.

God is calling for those who will go and stay even if in human eyes their work seems to be a failure. The missionaries to the Gold Coast of Africa in previous centuries used to take their coffins with them. At the best they knew that their life expectancy would be no more than two years. It was known as "the white man's graveyard", full of virulent diseases. They considered it a sacrifice well worth making. The blood of the saints freely given, has provided a seed bed for phenomenal growth in parts of Africa.

The Moravians who sold themselves into slavery were a living testimony of Jesus who stripped Himself of the glory of heaven to save a broken world. The cry of the nations is for people with that kind of heart and spirit.

In Acts 26:17-18 we read, "I will deliver you from the Jewish people as well as from the Gentiles to whom I now send you, to open their eyes in order to turn them from darkness to light and from the power of Satan to God, that they may receive forgiveness of sins and an inheritance among those who are sanctified by faith in me" (NKJ). These are great evangelistic verses. They emphasise the need for people to turn from darkness to light that they might receive forgiveness of sins. Yet in our desire to show people the ugliness of sin and to encourage them to turn from it, we often forget those simple words, "to open their

"Apostolic Passion
The term "passion" is used to describe everything from romance to hunger pangs. I don't know what it means to you, but for me passion means whatever a person is willing to suffer for. In fact that is the root meaning of the word. It comes from the Latin "passere" - to suffer. It is what you hunger for so intensely that you will sacrifice anything to have it. The word apostle means "a sent one" - a messenger. Apostolic passion, therefore is a deliberate intentional choice to live for the worship of Jesus in the nations. It has to do with being committed, to the point of death, to spreading His glory. It is the quality of those who are on fire for Jesus who dream of the whole earth being covered with the glory of the Lord"
Floyd Mc Clung.[14]

eyes". We read that the god of this world has blinded them to the truth. Unless people's eyes open they cannot respond. Firstly people need to know the difference between darkness and light, and secondly they need to recognise the need to pass from one to another. Cross-cultural mission is about finding "eye-openers", we see an example of this is Paul's life in Acts 17.

In Acts 17:23 Paul spoke with the people of Athens. He used the familiar altar as an "eye-opener". He pointed to the fact that the unknown god was the God Almighty of our Christian faith. He then tried to turn them from their idols. "To the weak I became weak that I might win the weak. I have becme all things to all men, that I might by all means save some" (1 Cor 9:22 NKJ). We don't just find "eye-openers" we can become one for the glory of God!

Hidden peoples who can only be reached through someone crossing a culture can be found in the streets where we live. Yet the vast majority of the un-reached peoples, Muslims, Buddhists, Hindus and tribal peoples live in the 10/40 window.

BLOG - MOUNTAIN PEOPLE

We set out on a journey to such a people hidden in the mountains of Africa. There has been intent to see Jesus become real amongst them, but little is visible after many years. Although He may have done more behind our religious backs than we know. It is illegal to witness openly and over the last 20 years no indigenous church has emerged in this people group of 4 million. To me this is an outrage, something has to happen, we would very much like to be involved in whatever small way He asks.

Once in the nation - miles of mountain roads and tracks with thousand of feet of rock falls, few vehicles travel these routes, the mountains sting with raw beauty, strong colours collide. Leave the vehicle, on foot now, the government will not easily release maps of these areas, We head for a village high in the mountains the furthest, highest one we can see. We catch glimpses in the clear air from miles below - before it disappears into the folds of the mountain. We are not very good at this wild wandering stuff - here because it seems to be an area that few are interested in and there is sickness and hunger, we know very little and will have to learn the language as we go. This will be our fifth language to work in on this journey - none of us are linguists.

We walk through villages that merge into the mountains contours, approach the gateway to the valley and head up into the strong heat. We want to hear him about how we enter, this has been a journey of hearing Him together. We are vulnerable in this and laugh a lot as we get things wrong and learn to trust and to take risks, sometimes leading I have to make the final call and trust it is the right one - sometimes there is no right one. We worship and pray a little in some shade, wash each other's feet, we want to enter, as it were clean from the journey, not bringing a crushing but walking as lightly as we can on our western feet. We wait for the village to come out to us and nervously they do, an older teenage lad "Abraham" meets us - we have no common language. We are welcomed and in time invited in, we pray for the sick, Jesus comes close and there is the beginnings of the joy and celebration we have seen before as the Kingdom breaks through. We learn mostly how much we do not know and do not understand. There is the disorientation of battery operated T.Vs and videos and a sense of an ebbing culture.

Approaching the highest village we take a wrong path and end up scrambling and exposed on a mountainside. Has the village disappeared? Was it ever there? Anxious now a few go ahead and in the distance we see the track and the houses stark against the rock. As we get closer there is a song that echoes on the thin air, a high sound from another way of being, as a young girl in a rainbow of colour, harvests a patch of green on a dusty slope. Later we meet and see that in some way we don't understand she is disregarded, rejected by the village. Is she barren, a rejected wife, young widow we don't know? It seems as if some recognise us, have they seen us in dreams? Again there is celebration and joy, again we pray for the sick in the name of Jesus, He comes in healing. Later some walk down in the darkness bringing others that have been missed. A toddler with badly burnt feet, women covered in sores - there is no healthcare here for the women and children. We experience the gospels firsthand, as the sick are brought to our door (for door read tents) it's good!

We camp outside. We would overwhelm the generous hospitality in a landscape where food is scarce. Days of travel, limits of language, cultural inadequacies though a desire to learn and to walk gentle - an extravagant waste of time and resources or simply a reflection of the extravagance of heaven?

From His perspective calling for the Kingdom to take root in unexpected ways does not seem to be a waste of time. Afterall Jesus spent the forty days after His resurrection teaching His disciples about the Kingdom of God. Maybe He was reminding them of the words He has spoken to them before His death when they were quietly asking Him about the sign of His coming and the end of the Age -"And this gospel of the Kingdom will be preached in the whole world as a testimony to all nations, and then the end will come" (Matt 24:14).

Many in the nations have no connection with His Kingdom. We say in our own culture that the best way for someone to become a Christian is through a friend. Many in the nations and in this nation will never have such a friend unless someone crosses a culture or even just crosses the street. Jesus, friend of sinners, is King in this area.

Can we see a movement of people raised up who will give themselves to this? The issue isn't how clever we are but rather how yielded we are to Him. It is time for pools and rivers - long term building and consistency alongside mobile teams who can flow spontaneously as He directs to people and places of need. Many in our nation have no connection with his kingdom, no connection with any expression of church because there is none within the community they belong to. It is time for a fresh mobility and pioneering alongside a depth of connection over many years - rivers and pools.

Even a small church like Antioch in Llanelli can play its part in community transformation. We can connect at many points of need, amongst broken young people, in areas of addiction, wrecked families and issues of employment. In all of this seeking through long-term building of relationship and care to create channels along which His love and power can flow. Whilst also releasing teams to flow to broken places and people in this nation and other nations.

It is also about pioneering in places where there has never been, or there is no longer an expression of church. It may mean pioneering amongst a marginalised or unreached people group in this nation or other nations. It is about doing what Paul did (Romans 15: 20). "It has always been my ambition to preach the gospel where Christ was not known, so that I would not be building on someone else's foundation". This surely is the greatest privilege.

There is a need to break the mindset of control, of Christendom, which developed in the church strongly from the time of Constantine. The journey to the margins amongst the poor shifts the locus of control. This control is also broken in releasing and empowering the congregation to be church, take church into the workplace and amongst friendship groups and people groups where there is connection. This can lead to the release of church developing naturally amongst culture. It can also mean choosing to make a long term cross cultural adaptation to another culture not your own, immersing yourself in it. Sometimes we lose the plot and the means by which we do things becomes an end in itself. A Kingdom focus helps us to focus!

"Instead of putting on a show and expecting everyone to come to us, the Organic Church takes the Kingdom to places where there are lost people and lives the Kingdom life among them and doesn't shy away from the gospel of the Kingdom. The lives that are drawn to Christ through that experience become the new church in that environment. As a result, they are immediately on board with walking with Christ and obeying him in the Great Commission and they become a catalyst for change in others and a chain reaction can occur. I think whenever you see a church planting movement, that's at the heart".15

Listen to this statement of intent by those seeking to live a new monasticism within the setting of third world slums - INCARNATION....We follow the pattern of Jesus who "though He was rich, yet for your sake He became poor, so that by his poverty we might become rich" (2 Corinthians 8:9), we commit ourselves to live and work among the urban poor, to live as nearly as possible to their standard of living, while maintaining reasonable health and recognizing emotional, physical, cultural and family limitations. We intend always to master the language and culture of the people amongst whom we minister".[16]

It is a crime against humanity that the church worldwide spends ninety percent of its resources on itself and only ten percent on the remaining half of the world; the half which has yet to hear the name of Jesus for the first time.

Is it possible for more finance to be released by the way we choose to live and give? Is it possible for wealthy people to choose a simple life-style for the sake of the gospel. The pioneer missionary David Livingstone said, "I will place no value on anything I have or may possess except in relation to the Kingdom of Christ".

A radical lifestyle means opening ourselves to the scrutiny of the Holy Spirit, not bowing to a cold legalism. Am I suggesting a dreary and grey way of living? No! It is our opportunity to experience in a fresh way Acts 2:42-47. An opportunity to discover the depth to which we love each other and the lost.

In the western church some of the oldest gods in history have emerged in an acceptable modern day form. A form with which we can feel comfortable - materialism, power, lust and status seeking. These are the very temptations with which Jesus was tempted. Radical lifestyle and radical community challenge all of this. God does put "the lonely in families" and a more communal style of living at whatever level we can enter it, certainly releases resource for the Kingdom. It can also give rise to a lot of fun and a lot of questions - more on community later!

"It would be real community in which competition was replaced by sharing....the needs of the poor would take priority in the economic decisions and ministry of the congregation. Living at a fraction of present lifestyle levels would become a natural way of life as compassion took root in community"
Jim Wallis.

TEN POOREST COMMUNITIES IN WALES.

The focus of some wild wanderings has been a series of journeys amongst the ten poorest communities in Wales - it has been a prophetic statement of God's intent and passion, an attempt to learn and to understand, a provocation to ourselves and others in a nation where many communities particularly poorer ones have no taste of the Kingdom, no living expression of church. This would also be true of Europe.

We used the Welsh Index of Multiple Deprivation to highlight the top ten poorest communities. The index exposes 'unmet needs', lack of resources and opportunities and includes data on income, employment, health, education, housing and access to facilities. The statistics used to complie this help us understand what it means to be "needy" in today's western world.

- Income - households receiving income support, family credit, disability allowance.
- Employment - unemployment claimants, incapacity benefit.
- Health - premature death, long-term illness.
- Education - adults with no qualifications, 16 + year olds
  not in full-time education, Key stage school test scores.
- Housing - % houses in disrepair, % without central heating.
- Access to services - distance to post office, large food
  shops, GP surgery, A&E unit.

"People can be considered to be deprived if they lack the material standards of diet and clothing, and do not participate in employment or recreation. If they lack the financial resources to obtain these conditions of life they are in poverty. It has be stated that while people experiencing some forms of deprivation may not all have low income, people experiencing multiple or single but very severe forms of deprivation are in almost every instance likely to have very little income and little or no other resources. So

deprivation depends on the level of conditions and activities experienced, and poverty on the incomes and other material resources available to the individual or household.

A distinction has also been made between material and social deprivation: people may not have material goods, facilities, or amenities. Additionally they may not have access to ordinary social relationships and activities. If there are these different forms of deprivation, then some people may experience several forms of deprivation and others only a single form."[17]

There is no one reason why certain areas make the top ten - they range from seaside towns to former coal-mining areas in the Valleys, and from relatively new council estates to old terraced housing. If you visit them you find they look quite different - some of them seem quite prosperous on the surface, others are obviously needy; some have a feel of community pulling together, others are struggling.

One common factor is that they are places that don't quite fit the twenty-first century - in many their whole reason for being no longer exists. The coal mines have closed; factories shut down; the holiday trade declined. There are few jobs around but people still live there - often in poor health, lacking qualifications and short of money.

The index was first produced in 2000. In most of these areas there is no viable church - although the situation is changing slightly.

In connecting with these areas we were not prayer walking although we were praying. We were looking for Holy Spirit connections with people - opportunities to share about Him, opportunities to pray for healing, and to learn, to receive as well as to give, to listen as well as to be listened to. It carries an immediacy and spontaneity, a flexibility to respond in the moment to a person and a need - no forms to fill out. In visiting these areas and numbers of others, we discovered hidden places and people who don't register on any lists. The Wildmill Estate in Bridgend seemed to be such a place.

Jen Hallet

BLOG - WILDMILL ESTATE, BRIDGEND

The Wildmill estate is a "hidden" place in that it does not show up as a specific area of need in any of the official statistics we could find. It is however, a poor estate with many needs. We met these two young lads, about 18 years old, and started to have a chat with them. We then asked them if they wanted prayer for anything and one of them asked if we could pray for his mum who had problems with her back and with walking. We prayed for her, and then one of them said that he had ended up in a police cell recently and that he was desperate and had been crying out to God to help. We prayed for him, and he said could we be quick as they thought the police nearby were after them!! We gave them the local church's address, and subsequently found out that one of them was in prison and was asking for contact with the church.

Zoe Britnell

It is in living in these places and going to these places (which in itself carries a powerful dynamic) that there is a clearer sight.

Rhyl West
- Victorian seaside resort on North Wales coast
- Large decaying terraced houses in multiple occupation
- Attracts people on benefit from the Merseyside area
- Very high incidence of drugs and crime

BLOG - RHYL WEST

Before we set out we prayed and looked at pictures- artistic representation of the "different faces of Jesus". Today I see anger in His face at the exploitation, the corruption of the fat cat landlords, the crime and violence, often drug and alcohol related. Have to deal with my own rage. There is a desperation here - lines of pain and hopelessness on faces - and the stories!

'Lizzie '(19?) just out of hospital, scar on throat where partner had tried to slit it. Missing part of her arm where she threw herself under a train. She is weak and ill, grateful for a cup of hot chocolate as she stands near a place where there seems to be dealing and prostitution happening. Pray for her before she is taken away by a man in an expensive car - where to? She seemed apprehensive and fearful. We are devastated. Something has to happen in this place.

'Alice' an alcoholic living in one room with two of her children and one grandchild.

INTEREST

The ten most deprived areas in Wales in 2000 were -
1. Rhyl West, Denbighshire.
2. Pen-y-Waun, Rhondda Cynon Taff.
3. Plas Madoc, Wrexham.
4. Gurnos, Merthyr Tydfil.
5. Maerdy, Rhondda Cynon Taff
6. Peblig, Gwynedd
7. Townhill, Swansea
8. Cymmer, Neath Port Talbot
9. New Tredegar, Caerphilly
10. Glanymor, Carmarthenshire

Gurnos, Merthyr Tydfil
- Large council estate in a declining industrial town
- High rates of unemployment and health problems
- Problems with crime, vandalism, drug and alcohol abuse.

BLOG - GURNOS

While on the estate we met a woman with two children and asked her if she wanted a food bag. She did, but didn't really want prayer, but said that her sister would want a food bag as well. Then she went her way and we continued walking around the estate. After a while we saw someone who looked just like the woman we had just given food bags to. We just started talking naturally to her and she knew we weren't from the estate and asked, "Are you the people giving out the food bags?" She was the sister of the person we had previously met. We replied "Yes", and she said that she had received the food bag and that nobody ever bothers to come to the estate to be kind. She wanted to know why we did that, and that simple act of kindness has amazed her. We said we just wanted to show that God is good, and asked her if she wanted prayer. She said yes and told us that she was a single mum with six children and one of them had cerebral palsy, couldn't eat through his mouth, and was confined to a wheelchair. We prayed for her and told her that God thought she was precious. She filled up with tears and we believe that God actually prepared the way through her sister, for us to meet her, and in turn, Jesus met her in a very real way.

Zoe Britnell

Glanymor, Llanelli
- Old terraced housing in a struggling industrial town
- Large elderly population
- High incidence of sexual abuse
- Drug and alcohol problems

BLOG - GLANYMOR

I saw this woman on the other side of the road, walking in the opposite direction and I could see depression on her. I asked her if she wanted prayer to be set free from drug addiction - she said yes. She was a single mum, whose husband was no longer alive due to a drug overdose. I prayed for her, and she started crying and then hugged me in the street and said that she had felt particularly low that day and was thinking what was the point of going on, but was encouraged that God had actually sought her out that day to tell her she mattered.

Maerdy, Rhondda valley
- Last town in the valley
- Built around coal mine which has closed
- Militant industrial history - known as "little Moscow"
- Many people with long-term health problems

BLOG - MAERDY

We headed up to the top streets of Maerdy and at the top, looked down the long and winding valley before carrying on our way. We met a man who was filling his car windscreen washer tank, explained what we were doing and he invited us into his house for a cup of tea. We talked with him and his wife. She had been suffering with depression and mental illness for years, you could see the pain in her eyes, albeit dampened down by the medication. We were able to give her time and attention to listen to her and pray for her and her husband and their family that Jesus would reveal Himself to her in the midst of her suffering and bring her healing. It was the simple goodness of God being left in their home through gifts, prayers and blessings.

We carried on downhill and met a mum, her teenage son and a neighbour sitting on the front wall and doorstep. They were passing the time of day with nothing better to do. We chatted with them, the neighbour had been out of work for a while and the mum was a single parent with all its challenges. The young man was full of nervous tension and a restless unease, one minute hanging on the door frame the next sitting on the step. They were happy for us to pray for them. I felt I should pray for the mum's financial problems (which surprised her as she hadn't mentioned money) and that the young man would be able to live out the dreams he had inside him, for the neighbour we called for job opportunities that would fit with his skills and abilities. We left them smiling, if not a little bemused.

Deb Chapman

In 2005 a new index was published based on smaller areas, and using better statistical data. This has produced a very different list which includes areas which did not appear in the first survey. In 2005 many of the traditional Welsh areas do better - this may be to some extent a result of the targeting of resources, but it also seems to highlight a new poor - the more recent incomers. Butetown has a large Somali poulation. Do we look after our own and ignore the strangers?

To see things change in these poorest areas of Wales (which are simply one reflection of the forgotten places and peoples of Western nations) will require focus. More than that it will involve the church emerging in new expressions across regions and cities. It will involve new levels of co-operation and interdependence.

INTEREST

Welsh Index of Multiple Deprivation 2005
Top Ten Areas

1 Butetown 2 , Cardiff.
2 Rhyl West 2, Denbighshire.
3 Penrhiwceiber 1, Rhondda Cynon Taf.
4 Penydarren 1, Merthyr Tydfil.
5 Twyn Carno 1, Caerphilly.
6 Castle 2, Swansea.
7 Penderry 1, Swansea.
8 Townhill 1, Swansea.
9 Queensway 1, Wrexham.
10 Rhyl West 1, Denbighshire.

It will involve long-term
determination and commitment
- not giving up - the release
of teams, circuit riding
for a new day. The release of a
wild army of the broken calling
in this new day.
It will require prayer...

Ask Him to help you. Enjoy prayer in all its colours and textures... "Prayer is not an activity, and it is not an application. It is life found in a person. Once you see Jesus, once the blindness falls away from your eyes in the glory of His presence, your attitudes about prayer will totally change." Jim Goll .[18]

These are just a few takes on prayer. Check out others mentioned in previous chapters -

Pray the Bible   - Pray the "Theophanies," Visions of God e.g. Ezekiel 1:28

The Psalms	- Life in the raw
Proverbs, Ecclesiastes	- Wisdom
Song of Songs	- Intimacy
Prophet's Prayers	- Crisis and revelation e.g. Ezekiel 37:1-14
The Prayers of Jesus	- e.g John 17:20-26
Hymns of Revelation	- Heaven's perspective e.g. Rev 22:12,17, 20.

Intercession   - "What is this thing 'identification in intercession' anyway? I believe that it is a lost art, and perhaps one of the highest, yet most overlooked, aspects of true intercession. It is the ability and function of personally identifying with the needs of others to such an extent that in heart you become one of them by the Holy Spirit" Jim Goll.[18]

Spiritual Warfare   - at it's most basic in lifestyle, word and confrontation - "Submit yourselves to God. Resist the devil, and he will flee from you" James 4:7.

Action -

• Take time to enjoy prayer as a relationship.

• Ask Him to help you explore facets of prayer you have never experienced before.

• Pray for the "least, the last and the lost".

Is Prayer Work?

There is a poem on prayer to be written
Cut into granite stone
Right words, right tools,
With craftsmanship
carved well.

Is prayer work?
A corporate hammering
a disciplined writing
on the hard rock of His will
Right prayer, right time
Right answer?

What about words unformed
In love's silence,
Words uncensored,
Coloured
Wrecked,
Thrown up on the mercy of His chest.

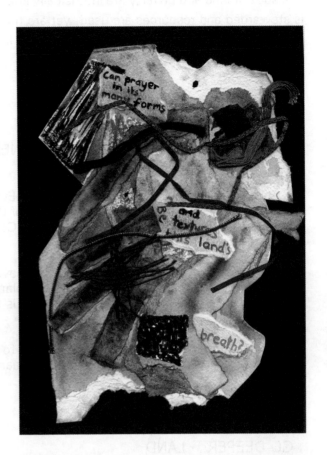

CONNECT WITH THE LAND

Dead end... hopeless... discarded places... discarded people... despair... isolation... loneliness... trapped... litter... burnt-out cars... graffiti... vandalism... drugs... crime... no-go area... debt...

Think of an area/street in your town which is like this... what would Jesus have done? Ask him what he wants to do now.

Jen Hallet

Issues of land and poverty are intrinsically linked. The poor often have little say in how land is stewarded and resources are used, yet are the most vulnerable in any disasters man-made or otherwise. In looking at spiritual aspects of land we also touch some of the more hidden roots of poverty.

GO DEEPER - STEWARDSHIP VS OWNERSHIP

In the garden the Lord said to Adam and Eve, "Be fruitful and multiply; fill the earth and subdue it. Have dominion over the fish of the sea, over the birds of the air and over every living thing that moves on the earth" (Genesis 1:28 NKJV). The land was given as a source and a resource.

Stewardship - recognises that what we have is a gift. We have a clear mandate to care for the environment, to look after the planet. Land is a resource to use wisely and hold with open hands. It's ours to share. This fosters a servant heart and openness to partner.

Ownership - believes that 'I have a right to what is mine' and 'I will do with it as I please'. This fosters an empire spirit and a fear to partner in case 'my' place of control, 'my' powerbase is lost.

GO DEEPER - LAND

This must be the desire of every community of believers that where they live becomes a place of open heaven - their town, village city, region, nation transformed - God redirecting its course and destiny.
Both Old and New Testaments teach us land is affected by the rebellion of mankind. There are 4 sins that wound, defile and pollute the land.

1. Idolatry

In Jeremiah 3:14, God pleads with His people to return to Him, 'for I am married to you.' To put any object or person before Him pollutes the land. He instructed the Israelites to pull down all the high places that other nations set up for false worship - they were to be His model that all nations were to see and copy as they turned to God.

2. Immorality

Our bodies are temples for God's Presence - the act of sex is an act of worship. It is a good gift for us to enjoy in the context of the marriage covenant and is a blessing. Leviticus 18:25 speaks of sexual sin defiling the land and that the punishment releases curse on the land and 'vomiting out'. Strong language!

An example from Llanelli: Machynys - Monks Island - is an area of land that had a monastery. The Abbot committed adultery and led an unsavoury life. The peoples of the area wanted the land back and a confrontation arose. The Abbot cursed the land and until recently, this land became a wasteland where nothing prospered.

In 2001, a small group of church leaders and believers from Llanelli came to that spot and identified the abuse of spiritual authority and immorality of that spiritual leader. Through identificational repentance and prophetic action, the land was cleansed. Four years later, the land has been reclaimed and a European golf course and housing development has been built, increasing the value of the land and bringing jobs to the poorest ward of the town. [Although I personally struggle with the fact that the gypsies were moved from this site, where they had been for many years, to another site where they didn't want to go - the injustice of this leaves me uneasy as to the roots we missed and maybe need to revisit - Karen].

3. Bloodshed

The shedding of innocent blood brings blood guilt on the land. Cain and Abel are a prime example of how jealousy and covetousness leads to murder. Abel's blood speaks from the ground, calling for justice (Gen 4:10). Bloodshed on the land through ungodly sacrifice whether it is the blood of animals or humans creates demonic strongholds on land.

An example from Indonesia: The Bali bombing of 2002 was not a terrorist incident which happened in isolation. It was a product of the past. British, American and Australian tourists were enjoying the nightlife of Bali clubs. These tourists were not aware that close to these clubs are mass graves with the remains of more than 80,000 Indonesians, mainly peasants who were murdered in Bali in 1965-66 with the silent and secret consent of the British, Australian and American governments. These peasants were communists fighting against the injustice of a dictatorial regime - General Suharto.

The clash of ideologies 'justified' motives of western governments who turned a blind eye to the dictator they armed as he 'cleansed the land' from opposition. The main casualties of the Bali bombing in 2002 were Australian, British and American tourists. The blood of the innocent cries out from the land.[19]

The following scriptures describe the principle of sowing and reaping on a personal and corporate level :-

Personally - 'Do not be deceived, God is not mocked; for whatever a man sows, that will he also reap' (Gal 6:7 NKJV)

Corporately - 'For the day of the Lord upon all nations is near; As you have done, it shall be done to you' (Obadiah 1:15 NKJV).

4. Broken Covenants

A covenant means a binding agreement between two parties. God is a covenant maker, His covenant is sealed by the blood of His Son. His covenant is Hs love in action and He set godly boundaries to keep us and the land in health and fruitfulness. Isaiah 24:5 says, "the earth is also defiled under its inhabitants because they have transgressed the laws, changed the ordinances and broken the everlasting covenant. (NKJV)

Consequences of Sins that defile the land

Deuteronomy 28 lists the blessings and curses that come through obedience and disobedience. The Bible lists four judgements that come upon the land as consequences of sin. They are :-

1. Famine - e.g. physical famine through drought; famine for truth (Jer 7:28); famine for His word.

2. Ecological disaster - e.g. flooding; earthquakes; tsunamis; hurricanes; acts of nature beyond man's control.

3. War - e.g. death, destruction, exile.

4. Disease - e.g. pestilence; physical disease affecting people or animals.

In his book 'Healing the Land', Winkey Pratney writes, 'Famine, ecological devastation, war and disease are four prophetic voices designed to get our attention when our moral madness is full. What we do not want to acknowledge will not be overlooked - that we cannot get away with living as if God does not exist or as if He has nothing to say to us.'

"How long will the land mourn and the herbs of every field wither? The beasts and birds are consumed, for the wickedness of those who dwell there because they said, 'He will not see our final end'" (Jer 12:4). Romans 8:22 describes these cries like this "the whole of creation groans and labours with birth pangs together until now". There is longing for a redemption yet to be realised.

There are times when walking the land, this groaning is picked up in your own spirit - you are 'hearing' the cry of the land.

Healing the land

The purpose of judgement is to bring us to our knees in repentance. The Biblical pattern for experiencing forgiveness and restoration includes four actions, confession, repentance, reconciliation and restitution. I am forgiven on the basis of my confession of faith in Jesus who is my sin-bearer and wound-taker. There is power in the blood and name of Jesus. As this is applied personally it also applies corporately.

The Cross is the place of reversal and restoration for territory as well as peoples. The Church is given the mandate to make known to principalities and powers in the heavenly realms the manifold wisdom of God. He is the Head and has taken His place on the throne of God. His last commission was for us to be His body and feet and take the gospel, this good news to all nations in His delegated authority. He has invested in us the power to confront the demonic realm, to heal the sick, to cleanse those with skin diseases, and to raise the dead. Sickness is one fruit of defilement on the land afflicting people.

Power confrontation = our powerlessness x His powerfulness

Ephesians 3 teaches us that it is our rooting and grounding in His love that fills us with the fullness of God. Simple really! Keep soaking in His love and His fullness is automatically carried in you wherever you go. No love - no fullness! Then Ephesians 1 states that the church is His body, the fullness of Him who fills all in all. We are born for this! WOW!

Community Transformation - a vision: heaven to earth

- Restored meeting place - stewarding His presence

- Restored stewardship - stewarding territory

- Heaven or hell on earth - you decide!

There are increasing numbers of islands and nations that are enjoying transformation where whole communities and governmental leadership are knowing the glory of God.

We will see increasing expressions of heaven or hell on the earth. Some of us are called to the places of hell, some of us are called to the places of stewarding transformation on the earth where the knowledge of His glory and His Presence are tangible.

We are called to make Him known, that none should perish but all come to the knowledge of God. Be blessed as you walk this out wherever He has called you!

Pip Gardner

WILD WANDERING

WILD WANDERING

PILGRIMAGE ...JOURNEY...TRAVEL...MISSION...PROGRESS...
PATH...SURVEY...ADVENTURE...WANDERING...

PEREGRINATIO PRO DEI AMORE...
WANDERING FOR THE LOVE OF GOD

Wild Wandering - why bother? Is it just adventure for adventure's sake or is there other purpose weaved within it? There is the wandering that takes us to desert places to encounter God in stark landscape where boundaries between heaven and earth are thin. Adventures to be had in the Spirit, crashed out on a bit of floor or sitting in an armchair.

There is a rhythm, wandering, flowing from a place of rest. Times of intense activity, connection with people flowing out of sheer pleasure in His presence in solitude and silence, time also to enjoy our humanity, enjoy our families, time to play and develop friendships. Ancient rhythms, walked out by Jesus can be lived out today,but it doesn't seem easy. Every breath we inhale is a token of His love for us, every breath we breathe out a token of our capacity to love in response, the rhythm of activity and rest is foundational yet activity often keep us, or at least me, from the very life that sustains.

The "peregrinatio" of the Celtic monks has been challenged from a modernist mind set as not 'proper mission'This misses the heart of what is a Spirit led dynamic. Their whole life

journey, at its best, flowed out of relationship with Jesus and from their contemplation and worship of the Trinity. It wasn't part of a twenty-first century "to do" list. It was the intentional and at times the unintentional overflow of the wonder of relationship with Him. So whether in the cell, in the desert, by foot or by coracle there was an overflow in their journeying which impacted the world around them - how could it not?

They were living what has been lived in other centuries also.

GO DEEPER - BIBLICAL BASE

In the Bible there are two types of wanderings; by judgement and by leading. The first type - judgement - we see in Adam and Eve leaving the garden, in Cain's exile, in the Tower of Babel and on one level in the wilderness wanderings of the 40 years. There is a kind of despair in this type.

The second type "leadings" can appear random but God is in them:

1. Noah wandering in a stationary fashion for 100 years, building an ark, then bobbing up and down at God's mercy for weeks and months.

2. Abraham's call and sojourn through Canaan.

3. Jacob fleeing but gaining an inheritance, learning about Bethel and Penuel, inheritance and birthright.

4. The whole story of Joseph.

5. Moses in Midian.

6. Wilderness wanderings - though in judgement there was still the presence of the Ark and the pillar that led them.

7. David and his journey - the psalms cast light on the devotional aspect, his spiritual and emotional journey.   The outcasts gathered to him in the cave at Adullam and became the "Mighty Men" their transformation happened as they joined David in the years of his journey to Kingship.

8. Elijah - began his journey, in fear, fleeing from Jezebel but was then sustained and led out.

9. Jesus, being filled with the Spirit, was led by the Spirit into the desert and came in the power of the Spirit to Nazareth.

10. Paul's missionary journeys.

Hywel Rhys Edwards

BLOG - FRANK LAUBAUN

MISSIONARY TO THE PHILIPPINES

Open Windows January 3, 1930, "I resolved that I would succeed better this year with my experiment of filling every minute full of the thought of God than I succeeded last year. And I added another resolve to - to be as wide open toward people and their needs as I am toward God, windows open outward as well as upward. Windows open especially downward where people need the most."

Feeling God in each moment: January 26 1930 "It means two burning passions: First to be like Jesus. Second to respond to God as a violin responds to the bow of the master. Open you soul and entertain the glory of God and after a while that glory will be reflected in the world about you and in the very clouds above your head".

Only one thing now: January 26 1930,"My part is to live in this hour in continuous inner conversation with God and in perfect responsiveness to his will. To make this hour gloriously rich". [1]

Wild wandering is not meant to be an escape born out of restlessness or a desire to avoid painful issues. The Book of Lismore (a medieval compilation of saints lives) identifies three kinds of pilgrimage. Pilgrimage without a change of heart made it a waste of time to leave country and home. For some true pilgrimage was staying at home because of responsibilities which made it impossible to make a physical journey. For others who were able to leave everything dear to them, for the right reasons, it was regarded as a high calling.

Peregrinatio was an outer journey that gave expression to an inner quest. It was a picture of the Christian life as repentance, rebirth and resurrection. It was a desire to experience the full dimensions of God in a literal journey that would be training and preparation for a heavenly home.

In the culture of that day the heroic was valued and the sacrifices made for a Heavenly King had to be more than those made for an earthly king. They had their eyes fixed on Jesus and their eyes fixed on the lost.

The desire to find a place of connection was at the root of much of the wild wandering, the 'peregrinatio', with which the Celtic Christians engaged. They saw it as a type of martyrdom.

The Celtic Christians embraced three types of martyrdom:

Red Martyrdom - literal death for the sake of Jesus. Some have said that they had it easy because there wasn't much of the red kind around! Maybe they were so good at converting the pagans they had to find other ways of living out extreme devotion!

White Martyrdom - seems to involve separation from everything that is loved including homeland; a focus on overseas travel with no returning.

It is confusing because Green Martyrdom seems almost identical but with the added extra of a separation from inner desires. It wears also the overtones of an imposed penance maybe for more serious sin issues.

Penance for the Celtic Christians seemed to be less of a punishment and more a series of redemptive steps required to bring change into damaged and sinful lives.

"The Penitential of Cummean (c.650) gives a list of twelve actions, beginning with baptism and ending with martyrdom, that are helpful in dealing with personal sin. This practical approach to faith saw permanent pilgrimage as a way of penance, not just to deal with past sins, but as a means of building a totally different way of living". [2]

Peregrinatio was radical commitment, "To leave one's home, never to return spoke of utter abandonment of self to a cause." [3]

GO DEEPER - ABRAHAM WILD WANDERING

SEVEN ULTIMATE TESTS

Abraham faced at least seven tests of faith in his years of wandering towards the land and future his Heavenly Father had promised.

- He knew all about the guidance test (Genesis chapters 11 and 12) - leaving the land he knew for the unknown.
- In Genesis 12:10-20 he experienced circumstances getting worse even when you obey - famine and, if people discovered his identity, a death threat.
- Would you have got someone close to lie to save your life - or trust in God's protection? The integrity test.
- He allowed Lot to have the first choice of a place to settle - preferring him to himself and trusting God for the difference (Genesis 13;1-18).
- Then rescued Lot when he was captured by the four kings - spiritual warfare.
- The greatest test of faith - delayed promise (Genesis 16). Years rush by and still no son of promise.

- And then the ultimate sacrifice (Genesis 22: 1-19) trusting for resurrection, trusting for promise to be fulfilled.

The verdict on Abraham? Hebrews 11:8-12
"By faith Abraham, when called to go to a place he would later receive as his inheritance, obeyed and went, even though he did not know where he was going. By faith he made his home in the promised land like a stranger in a foreign country; he lived in tents, as did Isaac and Jacob, who were heirs with him of the same promise. For he was looking forward to the city and foundations whose architect and builder is God. By faith Abraham even though he was past age - and Sarah herself was barren- was enabled to become a father because he considered him faithful who had made the promise. And so from one man and he as good as dead, came descendants as numerous as the stars in the sky and as countless as the sand on the seashore".

CONNECT WITH
THE POWER OF A SHORT JOURNEY

Columba's journey from the coast of Derry with 12 companions in 563 whether it was exile, penance or mission or simply the combination of all three in peregrinatio led him to the island of Iona and the establishment of one of the greatest missionary centres of the Celtic church.

TAKE A SHORT JOURNEY AND SEE WHAT HAPPENS

One of the most familiar stories of a wild wander is the one mentioned in the year 891 in the Anglo-Saxon Chronicle[4] which tells how three Irishmen came to Cornwall in a curragh, without any steering oar, 'because they wanted to go into exile for the love of God, they cared not whither'

The wandering of the Celtic saints took them all over the continent and beyond, as far afield as Russia, the Slavic peoples, Iceland, Switzerland, Austria, Northern Italy, as well as the France, the Low countries and the Rhine Valley.

We can still follow their trail into Europe.

CONNECT WITH EXTREME

Do Extreme, stir up the adventurer in you , practice listening to and following the Holy Spirit.

Go to an airport taking a limited amount of money buy a cheap return flight to somewhere in Europe - go with someone, consult with others and pray, ask Him where you should go and what He wants you to do - then go.

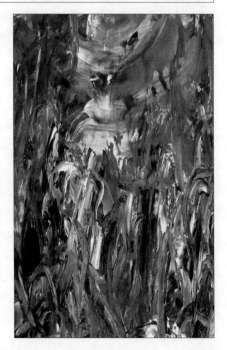

Europe is a continent crying out for resurrection, maybe as much of a challenge as the 10/40 nations. It is a continent of un-reached people groups accessible in cities, the hidden poor and those exploited in economic and sexual slavery.

Europe is also a continent where the church is rapidly dying and the culture is ravaged with materialism and immorality, isolation and fear.

Europe has been described as burnt ground, "waves of biblical, Holy Spirit Christianity spreading across Europe, yet being extinguished again and again in our history. Burnt ground describes the difficulty of recovery. Wherever fire has passed over ground it consumes everything that would provide fuel for any other fire... Yet we believe in corporate grace. It is these earlier fires that represent our heritage and spiritual inheritance. It is our conviction that no living word prophesied, no life laid down whether living or dying and no prayer prayed are ever lost, rather they are ours to be regained".[5]

Wild Fire Revival

Thought wild fire revival
Would be lightning strikes of power
on tall trees
pushing against the skyline.
Futures ignited
abandoned to His hot-flame love.

Thought wild fire revival
would leap policed camps of the Church
torching underground movements
the Holy Spirit is already enjoying
behind our straight
religious backs.

Thought wild fire revival
would be His breathing
on cold embers in the Nation's hearth
generations welded in His heat.

It has so far, not been so.
We have become a crucible of burning,
goodness gone, dreams charred sticks,
sin-stark strikes of pain.
A Beachhead slaughter,
casualties, and within, the fifth column
of pained reactions.

Are we a land to be corrupted by ash
or nourished?
A robbed or cleared ground springing
Life?
Seeds long dead rejected or ignited in Europe's ground?
Let us be a new day
lit in the terrible fire of ruthless love
Shadowed with ash that marks the land's face
        With strange beauty.

HISTORY - WHITBY

AD664 - The disastrous *Synod of Whitby* "brings order" to the growing differences between the Celtic Way and the Roman Way by enforcing Roman regulations about the date of Easter and monks' haircuts(!). Cuthbert and Hilda accept these to preserve unity but maintain a Celtic spirituality. The regulations from Rome are accepted in Northern Ireland in 696, in Scotland in 716 and in Wales in 755.

It is a continent where seed long buried in the land await fresh life, twenty-first century expression.

PULLING UP THE ROMAN WAY

"These are huge days. The world has changed and the Lord is looking for those who are without fear. Steve Lowton is preparing to walk from Whitby to Canterbury and then Canterbury to Rome. These walks absolutely connect prophetically with our destiny". Martin Scott.

"I write this with news of the arrest of the last London bomber ringing in my ears. Arrested in Rome it is as if the Lord is signalling so strongly that that the paths of oppression and injustice have to be walked and prayed for. Rome is without doubt the most visible symbol of Christendom within the western world. We the church have to own the appalling damage that the centuries of Christendom has done to the reputation of the gospel and the name of Jesus. So why are we walking?

• To take note of the sign given when the bombers of July 7th were discovered to have come from Leeds; a "first city"[6] that was prophesying a strong warning to the nation of England and the nations of Europe of what is to come if a place of deep repentance is not found.

• To repent for the sins of Christendom and Empire that dominates the landscape of Europe, some of its bitter fruit it could be said we are tasting through the appalling work of the bombers.

- To call for the rolling up of the ways of Empire that the Roman war machine represents; in its place calling for the wild wind of the Holy Spirit to be loosed across our continent and for grassroots movements of the people of God to rise".

This is a declaration that a young prophet from Leeds has written for me in preparation for our arrival in St. Peters Square on the shortest day of the year; Dec 21st, 2005. At midday we will gather there to conclude the walk. My hope is that wherever you are you will feel able to join us as we make this declaration together.. We are back on the walk on Dec 12th with 480 km remaining. Rome is in sight!" Steve Lowton

Our Declaration: We declare Lord that we are impressed with You, Your Kingdom, Your Ways. We refuse to be impressed with Empire, or impressed with Rome. We declare a breaking down of every throne which exalts itself against You Lord, a putting down of the mighty, a raising up of the meek; we are looking for a throne founded on righteousness and justice. We bring with us days of throne breaking. We have no Caesar but Christ! To all you Roman ways which arch across Europe, we prophesy your pulling back, we shut you down, we speak a breaking, a winding down and a rolling up of all your lines of control. We pull you back and out of these lands and bring to bear every step and syllable of prayer against your hold and dominion. We cancel every unclean decision made in Whitby and pull a new heavenly legislation across our continent. We declare the Wild Wind and Ways of God into your midst. We call for the rising we look to the horizon for, the breaking of boxes and a Kingdom coming into European places. We call a greater Kingdom down! Empires break and slave nations go free! To the people of God, we declare a day of liberty, of Jubilee, we declare days of the exodus, days of running free - we say pyramids and towers can stay unfinished; we go looking for our lands of promise! Because of the mandate of the great commission to go, we who have walked the other way say that 'temple, we will no longer serve you'; we go from Jerusalem to Judea and to the ends of the earth! On the shortest day, we proclaim a shortening of Roman days and the lengthening of New ones. Into this twilight day of daylight turning, we rebuke fear and make a choice and pray for life. We call for and bless the days when hidden decisions find grace far wider than imagined, and where lepers put armies to flight. We call for days of siege breaking in the midst of twilight and the fleeing away of empires which have starved our places of sight, our places of vision. Flour and Barley for a Shekel in the gates of Samaria! Sight in the places of seeing. Empire, begin to ship out! No more! New days, new risings, new anointing, more-ancient ways, stronger words, deeper senses, further sight. We pull tomorrow in through the Spirit of Prophesy within us, we call the Testimony of Christ in. Caesar, your testimony is dismissed! Lord breathe your words into Europe. So we loose the sounds of the trumpet, sounds of the new year and of slaves going free. Let the sound of breaking thrones fill heaven's gates. We call earth and heaven's hosts to bear witness to a breaking on the shortest day. We bear witness to new days coming through, of exodus, of people walking another way, of old sieges lifting and ancient promises finding space in these lands. Let old prayers find days of answer, Lord. So we place again this window of grace into Your hands. We hand You six months of seeking for scalpel, of declarations of sword and of agreements by prophets. We place them before You as these days close and call for change across this corner of creation. Complete what You have started. We give You Glory Lord, every step and breath is yours, as ever. We love You. Amen. [Steve is now planning to walk from Rome to Jerusalem].

CONNECT WITH WILD WANDERING

Go on a Wild Wander

- Focus on the poorest places you can find and gain a sight of what this 21st century expression of His Kingdom and His life might look like in a European context.
- And if you dare lay down your life to see it outworked.

CHRIS' BLOG - EUROPE AND THE DAY TO DAY

By Easter 2005 I was tired. The past months had been busy. I had been working freelance as a video cameraman and pursuing the kind of lifestyle I thought I had wanted.

I'd left university 2 years ago with great dreams of living as some kind of urban monk, earning my money for the week with one day's camera work and spending the rest of my time travelling around and praying in different cities. This had happened for perhaps the first year, after which time I had felt the need to invest more time in my work. I felt a sense of loss. I felt that I had reneged on some of my former dreams, and I didn't see how to return to them.

And then Road Trip happened.

In Easter 2005, my friend Andy told me about a trip he was organising that summer. For a long time he and a mate had been carrying a vision to travel up the west coast of Europe preaching the Gospel and praying for the continent. This year, he said, they were putting their plan into action - and did I want to go? The moment he had told me about it I knew it was somehow important. I just had a feeling. I told him so, and said I'd love to go but there was no way I could afford it. He suggested I come along and make a film about it, and he'd pay for my ticket. I thought about it for all of 10 seconds before agreeing.

I met up with the team in Faro, Portugal. Some I knew already while others were complete

117

strangers. We were a young group: several students, a couple of youth workers, a pair of surf addicts and a handful of random others. Of the thirteen of us, only three spoke any of the relevant languages we were likely to need. The plan was fairly simple: we would travel up the west coast of Europe through Portugal and Spain into France. Along the way we would stop at various points to pray and seek opportunities to preach the Gospel.

From the very outset our journey was everything you might expect from a road trip. With the windows down and the music blaring, we meandered our way up the coast. Andy, map in hand, led us to our various stopping points: beaches, towns, mountainsides and clifftops. Each stop was an opportunity to see something new, to pray, and to do our best to engage people in conversation. We had hundreds of little red "Road Trip" gospel tracts - in Portuguese, Spanish, French and English. Through the course of the journey these leaflets managed to find their way into the most unlikely of hands. Surfers received them on the beaches; tourists were given them in the towns. Bar and café owners took them with varying degrees of interest and/or suspicion. In one town we returned to our vehicles to find them being towed; after a lively negotiation to get them released, three of our number managed to give a tract to each of the three traffic wardens that had been about to impound our car.

I have to be honest, I've never been the world's biggest fan of tracts. But in this situation, where the language barrier was a constant obstacle, they proved an excellent way of communicating. If people were interested then they would be willing to continue the conversation despite the extra effort required to overcome the linguistic difficulties. If they weren't interested, then at least they could understand and make an educated decision to walk away.

Early in our travels we visited the most south-westerly point of Europe and sat on the very tip of the land, looking out across the Atlantic Ocean, praying over all the countries stretched out beyond. We camped on the cliff top overnight, cooking fish on an open fire and sharing communion under the stars. As we watched the rising moon reflecting on the water it was easy to see how that very spot had inspired so many missionaries before us. It's hard not to trust a God that created all that, and it's difficult to remain proud in the face of such beauty. Out of all the great moments of the trip, that evening stays in my mind. Sleeping on the rough ground in such a weather beaten spot, I felt like I was connecting with something old that had been lying dormant in me for too long. And it was this feeling that I was to bring home with me, that inspires me still. But more on that later.

In my own naïve way, I felt at times that God wasn't really showing up in the way I'd like Him to. We didn't see any huge shiny miracles, and we have no idea what difference our prayers have made to the lands we prayed over. But there were many ways in which God chose to surprise us.

In Lisbon we met four lads from Italy and felt we should have prayed for them but had all missed the moment. We prayed that more Christians would come into their path as they continued their travels. That ended up being us when we met up wuth them again in Porto. One of them, Allesandro, was visibly touched by what one of the team had prophesied over him.

While our trip wasn't marked with astounding miracles (even the sore throat we prayed over resolutely refused to be healed!) it was infused with moments such as this. One girl on the team had a dream one night about a lad she used to know as a child, someone she hadn't even thought about for years. The next day she bumped into him in the street. She had the opportunity to talk through her faith with him and to share something of the Gospel. It seemed that while we had been planning our route, God had been planning the people we would meet along the way. We don't know how deeply any of those people were impacted by God as a result of our meetings; certainly none made an instant confession of faith. But God was so clearly and literally guiding our footsteps that I feel confident that He has seen to it that his purposes have been achieved.

In the aftermath of Road Trip, I began to reflect on the things I had experienced. Lying on that clifftop at the start of our trip, I had felt more alive than at any time I could remember over the previous year. After only three weeks, I had grown to love that wild lifestyle. I loved the spontaneity of it, and I loved the way it forced you to make a choice: worry, or trust God. Even after such a short space of time, I returned to my flat in the UK and found that my own comfortable-ness itched like a rash I couldn't get rid of. I found it difficult to sleep in my bed knowing that tomorrow would be much like the day just gone. I realised that in most areas of my life - my work, my relationships, my leisure time - I had successfully eliminated all the elements of risk. I was left safe, but unfulfilled.

Road Trip had reminded me of what made me feel alive: living by the wild wind of God's spirit, relying on God for provision in all areas, and trusting Him when it comes to taking the opportunities He presents. But I was left with a question in my mind. It's fine living like that when you're on holiday with no responsibilities, but how does that work back in "real life"? How do I live by the wild wind of the spirit here and now in 21st Century England - especially when I know God has called me to work in the media (which means actually working and not just earning enough to fund my prayer habit)?

I still don't think I've got all the answers. But the more I think about it, the more convinced I am that "living by the wild wind of the spirit" isn't primarily about putting your walking boots on and going out into the wilderness to sleep under the stars. As Road Trip reminded me, I delight in that stuff and it is always a wonderful reminder of what it means to follow God in the wild ways. But there must be an attitude of the heart that runs deeper than those surface outworkings. And that attitude has to be the one modelled so effectively by Jesus. He didn't care about man-made structures or empires; He didn't do what people told him and gave no regard for the way He "should" do things. The only thing He cared about was doing what He saw the Father doing.

And so as I reflected on my own life, I began to see things differently. I had been praying about my work one day, asking God all of these questions and more, when it began to dawn on me that in so much of what I was doing, I had been investing my time doing the things I thought everyone else said I should be doing. I had cut my hair short, I had smartened up a little, and I had begun to try and think like a young entrepreneur. Particularly in my dealings with others in the industry, I had tried (and probably failed) to project an air of slick professionalism. I wasn't dealing with people as people, I was dealing with them as contacts and colleagues. I was trying to be something I wasn't. But praying that day, I felt God remind me that I don't need to live by these rules I set for myself. He said to me, "Just make friends". Not, "be more professional", or, "be more organised". Just make friends. From that point I started to look at the people I was dealing with differently. Where I had been slightly afraid of them before (What will they think of me? Will they give me work? What if I screw up?), I started to relax around them. After all, all I was interested in was making friends with them. Funnily enough, I've just started a new job with a TV production company. And how did I get that job? Because I made friends with a guy who happens to be director of the company I'm now working for, and when an opportunity came up he offered it to me. Simply making a friend has taken me out of my home town into a new environment, and has given me the opportunity to more fully follow the call of God on my life.

For me, living by the wild wind of the spirit is about being open. Being open to where God takes you, and being open to the people he introduces you to. It's about being able to see the God-ordained opportunity in every situation, and trusting God enough to take it - even when it might mean risking something. It means not worrying, but trusting that it's God who's directing your path. It means allowing things to happen accidentally (as far as you're concerned) but realising that they have been intended since the dawn of time by the loving Father. And it means not doing things because everyone else says that's the way it should be done, but doing them because you're following the finger of God.

Who knows where it could all lead? Not me. But I know that I can trust Him.

Chris Stone

GO BY SEA

BRENDAN'S PRAYER

"Shall I leave the prints of my knees on the sandy beach, a record of my final prayer in my native land? Shall I then suffer every wound that the sea can inflict? Shall I take my tiny coracle across the wide sparkling ocean? O king of the Glorious Heaven, shall I go of my own choice upon the sea? O Christ will you help me with the wild waves?" [7]

HISTORY ~ BRENDANS VOYAGE

This is an extreme wild wander from Ireland ~ It has to be Brendan! Tim Severin proved in the late '70's that it was possible to sail a boat similar to Brendan's sixth century curragh all the way to America along the same route Brendan would probably have taken.

Brendan's story holds echoes of the different Atlantic Isands he could have encountered on the journey. The "hot rock" that pelted Brendan and his monks ~ the volcanoes of Iceland; the islands of sheep ~ the Faroes; the white cloud ~ the fog zone on the Great Banks of New Foundland just before the "Promised lands" ~ intriguing stuff.

Brendan was born in Ireland sometime around AD 489 in Co. Kerry Ireland near Tralee. He was an apostolic strategist who established strong teaching and sending monastic centres His name is connected with the foundation of settlements in Kerry, Galway and Clare. One of the most famous of these in Galway was at Clonfert where the story of "the voyage of Saint Brendan" begins.

" Saint Brendan, therefore, when fourteen brothers out of his whole community had been chosen, shut himself up in one oratory with them and spoke to them saying:

'From you who are dear to me and share the good fight with me I look for advice and help, for my heart and all my thoughts are fixed on one determination. I have resolved in my heart if it is God's will ~ and only if it is ~ to go in search of the Promised Land of the Saints of which Father Barrind spoke. How does this seem to you? What advice would you give?

They, however, having learned of the holy father's will, say, as it were with one mouth:

'Abbot, your will is ours. Have we not left our parents behind? Have we not spurned our inheritance and given our bodies into your hands? So we are prepared to go along with you to death or life. Only one thing let us ask for, the will of God.'

Saint Brendan and his companions, therefore decided to fast for forty days ~ but for no more than three days at a time and then to set out...

"Then the holy father with his group was driven here and there for three months over the space of the ocean. They could see nothing but sky and sea". After many adventures, strange sea creatures, demonic attacks, hails of fire and rock, the deaths of some of the monks and many strange islands, they came to a " whole land and could not find the end of it".

But one day they came upon "...a great river flowing through the middle of the island. Then Saint Brendan said to his brothers: 'We cannot cross this river and we do not know the size of this land.' They had been considering these thoughts within themselves when a youth met them and embraced them with great joy and, calling each by his name, said

'Happy are they that live in your house. They shall praise you from generation to generation.'

When he said this, he spoke to Saint Brendan:

'There before you lies the land which you have sought for a long time. You could not find it immediately because God wanted to show you his various secrets in the great ocean. Return, then, to the land of your birth, bringing with you some of the fruit of this land and as many of the precious stones as your boat can carry. The final day of your pilgrimage draws near so that you may sleep with your fathers. After the passage of many times this land will become known to your successors, when persecution of the Christians shall have come. The river that you see divides the island. Just as this land appears to you ripe with fruit, so shall it remain always without any shadow of night, for its light is Christ.'

Saint Brendan with his brothers, having taken samples of the fruits of the land and of all its varieties of precious stones, took his leave of the blessed steward and the youth. He then embarked in his boat and began to sail through the middle of the fog". [8]

INTEREST - CURRAGHS

"From now on all Columba would ever want would be a small ship and a star, the word of God on his cheek... He would strive to become the least of men indistinguishable from those who pulled the oar with calloused hands." First nation peoples are often associated with canoes, coracles and curraghs. They are recorded as used and even still being used in some of these nations:

Galacia to Greenland Armorica (Brittany), Cornwall, Wales, Ireland, Blaskets, Aran, Achill, Inish Kegs, Inish Bofin, Tory, Hebrides, North Rona Flannen Island, Orkneys, Shetland, Faroes, Vestmann Island, Iceland.

Father Kelly of the people of Inish Whale "If they couldn't get a curragh launched, "the living starved and the sick died."..."the sorrows of the poor are as tragic as the fate of ancient heroes."

Tomás - Blasket Islands "It was our business to be out in the night and the misery of that sort of fishing is beyond telling, I count it the worst of trades."

"There is a spirituality in the people that one notices....one reason for this is that the people of the islands live in proximity to the elements, to the sea, to the danger of their being drowned, to the dangers of airplanes, the dangers involved in fishing, to the dangers of gales, storms and to the high seas of winter". On a voyage in high and dangerous seas Padraig Standún writes:

"Ar lá marsin a chuirteé curach I grosúlacht le brág chrior ag siúl ar an bhfamaige - On such a day you imagine the curragh as the shoe of Christ walking the sea". [9]

The water is an island people's desert you can die of thirst in both.

GO BY CANOE.

Three years ago I had this idea of kayaking right around Wales. No-one had done it on their own before and I wanted to do it partly as a prayer journey.

In my heart, the trip had two main aspects....one was the whole prayer journey side and the other was as a fund raising event to help AIDS orphans in Kenya. I thought that I would enjoy it too! It seems that God also enjoys the adventuring/exploring side of who I am. I saw it creating a 'prayer slick' around Wales which seems appropriate as I'm not a great intercessor! I sensed that even if I wasn't constantly praying, I would be carrying His presence as I paddled.

The journey itself began on Llandudno beach at 6.30 p.m. on June 1st 2003 and I set off on to the calm sea with prayers of blessing from my church and family. The distance ahead of me was about 580 miles , which I thought would take me three weeks, though it only took two in the end. I headed East along the North Wales coast then up the Dee estuary as far as Chester. I then joined the canal system and followed this South, as close to the Welsh border as possible, emerging onto the river Severn and then working my way back out to sea and North to my starting point.

I decided to do the trip solo because things become less complicated that way and it's easier to get into a rhythm of paddling and daily life.

Once on my way, the feel of the praying changed. I thought that maybe I would be disciplined enough to pray at regular intervals during the day, but no , it wasn't quite like that. Singing the Psalms became one of the easiest and most meaningful things to do . As I was averaging over 11 hours of paddling each day, I had plenty of time for singing as well.

I would try to memorise bits of the Psalm that I had read that morning and then sing out of that.The seagulls seemed to enjoy it anyway!

However, beyond what I was doing or singing or praying, there was just a sense that God was there, with me and in me. I believe there was something of Joshua 1:3 going on... " I will give you every place where you set your paddle! "

There are aspects of a long journey that complement the spiritual life ... there is a simplicity about it; a sense of rhythm and focus that draw you in. There is a transience about it too, of not settling in one place, moving on every day, with God.

The added dimension that sea kayaking brings to the journeying is one of working with forces supremely bigger than oneself... of having to wait for the tidal streams to run in the right direction, of working with the currents and not against them, of only going out to sea when the wind and waves allow for that to happen safely.

There were a couple of days in the middle of the trip when I could not go any further because of the strong winds. I had arrived at Port-Eynon on the Gower and had pulled up on to the beach for my regular six hour break to wait for the tide to turn again in my favour. However, during that time the weather began to worsen and the sea to roughen. I called the coastguard on my VHF radio for a weather check and he warned me of unsettled weather for the next forty-eight hours.

Once the strong winds had eased off a bit I headed out to sea again and felt refreshed enough to tackle the first of the long open crossings , from Worm's Head to Caldey Island; a distance of over fifteen miles. This committing crossing felt very exposed amid some of the biggest seas I had paddled in, waves of twenty feet to twenty-five feet high. There were no simple short-cuts if anything went wrong out here. It felt like mountaineering in a kayak; one minute climbing up steep glistening ravines with scalloped walls then the next, sliding down into blue earthquaking valleys. With no sight of land ahead I had to simply trust my compass bearing and press on.

Five hours later I was glad to reach the sanctuary of Caldey, though I think all the monks had already gone to bed. It had certainly been a day of wild wandering!

The long open crossings were a highlight for me. I had to do two of fifteen miles,one of twenty-eight miles (Tywyn-Aberdaron) and one of thirty-five miles (Aberdaron-Treaddur). Some would say that once you've done one, then what's the point ? To me, being miles out at sea on your own, with the only glimpse of land a thin slither on the horizon is exhilarating. It's like a step of faith; scary and yet exciting at the same time, a revealing of who you are...pretty small, but of significance too; doing your bit, are we really making progress? ... I know my destination is over there even though I can't see it yet ... don't give up .God, I'm in your hands!

..The whole journey, essentially, was like being carried. Though I did the paddling, the water held me up and, often, almost imperceptibly, propelled me forwards".

Steve's Equipment List -

Kayak - 2 ft wide and 17ft long
Hand pump - "If I'm out at sea and the boat collapses, there is a technique called re-entry and roll where I get back into the kayak, use the paddle to get upright, then use the pump to get the water out - that's the theory!"
Spare pair of paddles - vital in case I drop one at sea.
A VHF radio and emergency location beacon and buoyancy aid "In case I get thrown out".

Steve Porter

GO BY FERRY

Sunday May 15th

Got to Swansea port, thinking how spiritually unprepared I am and praying that the next couple of days won't just be a 'nice' trip but a trip of God's anointing and interaction.

At the terminal. Before I could sit down an American guy, mid to late twenties asked, "Where are you going?" So I moved my bags next to him, trying to show him that I've got the time and interest to speak to him. Was speaking to him quite freely and ensuring that I didn't miss out the whole reason I was on this journey, God. As I started to chat to Matt, I was beginning to be impressed by his own adventure and how he was engaging in the whole simplicity of monastic journey. Like when he turned up at Swansea train station a few days before and slept in the staff quarters. This happened by asking for help and guidance from a train guard. He had also knocked on someone's door to ask permission to set up camp in their back garden.

Inspiring stuff, I could learn stuff from this guy, I thought, Matthew 7:7 came to mind. Finally I boarded the ferry, found out the best seats were in the pub at the front. Most of the large half moon shaped seats were taken, except for one where a lady in her mid-30's was sitting by herself. Dressed up like a proper tree-hugger, she immediately radiated what you see is what you get. Suzie mentioned amongst many other activities that she regularly does some kind of palm-reading-come fortune telling, via computer software to many people. She mentioned that most of her clients were elderly people and how she loves holding their hands and wondering when was the last time this person had their hand held - ouch! Need wisdom to know what to do and what to say ...

I started climbing a hill to one edge of Cork. Just wanted to look over Cork and declare this is God's territory and ownership. Got completely lost and was quite annoyed. Kept thinking, hoping and praying - will I actually meet someone where I could really pray into their life? To be honest I was feeling a bit nervous and faith-less. The place was polluted by both noise and smell, the view also wasn't much to write home about. Was moaning to God, why on earth have you brought me here? I can't even hear myself think!

But felt God saying, don't be driven by surroundings, I'm here no matter what conditions. On that I notice a guy pacing up and down kicking grass and rubbish. So I approached him, noticed he had a cut on his nose, looked quite rugged and I said a usual ice-breaker, "A bit noisy isn't it." I just started talking to him. He soon became more relaxed as he was telling me about his life, every now and then he would almost square up to me getting very close to my face. But I honestly wasn't afraid of this guy who could obviously look after himself. The cut on the nose was from the result of a punch up he had in the pub the night before.

Paddy was so hurt and defeated spiritually. Split from his wife and kids back in England, lived with his sister, but she didn't speak to him. Has Parkinson's disease and is addicted to gambling, spending all his money in the bookies within the first hours of getting his giro. He shared a little bit about his family, two of them on the run after escaping from prison. Had no spark of hope, poor lovely Paddy I was thinking. But within ten minutes here we were laughing together, talking about life and God. After about an hour I asked if I could pray for him. Boy, I've never felt so authorised to pray for someone just off the street like I felt with Paddy. Afterwards he asked me if I'd interpret a dream and a nightmare! Genuinely felt a lot of love for this guy and just asked God to enter his life. Me being me, I wanted to leave him with something practical as well. I only had a packet of biscuits, so I gave them to him, he was well chuffed with them too!

Tuesday May 17th
Woke up this morning pretty excited just on the fact of spending another day (trying) to be directed by the Lord. I didn't want to assume that being directed by the Lord meant doing something extraordinary but trying to be extraordinary in the normality. It doesn't sound much but actually just giving time to people to be heard, which normally means someone having an ear to moan at.

Wednesday May 18th
I decided to walk around town and started to pray, asking God to connect me with anyone who He wanted me to approach. I saw a street guy crouched up against a huge glass window of a café, drinking from a beer can, you could see a group of people just sitting chatting, sipping on their drinks. I thought, what a picture, then it dawned on me how I just automatically passed this guy, knowing his situation. I stood there asking the Lord if He wanted me to speak to him and my weakness of flesh kicked in, thinking what happens if he tells me to get lost and everyone in the café laughs at me, or what happens if he goes for me and I end up in hospital and miss my ferry!! Then I thought sod this, just give me a sign if you don't want me to speak to him and approached the guy. But as I got closer I noticed that he was speaking on a mobile phone! And took this as a sign. To be honest, this well could have been a cop out and was a little angry with myself for being a coward!!

 By this time I was needing a bit of a rest and thought about going to the cinema. Found one and booked a ticket to see a film in a couple of hours. Lunch time was due and I ended up in a fast food joint, a first for a few months. As I sat munching a man sat down a couple of tables away. He had saliva all down the front of his jumper, then every two minutes or so he'd go into an compulsive shake sending his saliva all over the place. A few people moved away to further tables. I knew I had to act but weren't sure too sure the appropriate way. Was trying to hear from God, but was a little impatient so opened up the Bible and asked God to give me inspiration and instruction. It opened to Matthew 7: "Stop judging others, and you will not be judged. For others will treat you as you treat them."

Ok, so You want me to imagine me being him and what would I want then? Well at least something to wipe all that spit I thought. So I just plonked the serviettes on the table, whilst dodging the flying spit, then popped to the loo. As I walked passed him I saw him wiping his chin. I know I could have done more but doing the very little I did, probably the least, my heart was filled with joy. I walked around praying for that man and thanking God for him and the opportunity.

Reflecting back on the day so far felt it was quite testing. I was naturally tired today what with the rain, the drunk, Mr Dribbler. How I always want to do things on my terms, when it suits and fits me. As soon as something a little uneasy comes up, how quick I am to quit. Don't get me wrong, this wasn't on a condemning side but more an actual fact/ observation side - that is how much fear and self preservation I work on.

Finally got to the port for the ferry and there were about 4 people there, one being a guy looking like a New Ager. I instantly knew that I'd be talking to him. So I just went up and spoke to him. I think the strange thing was how quickly the conversation was on to religion. He was a goddess worshipper. I felt it was my time to ask him questions, like does he believe in Jesus?

Next morning arriving in Swansea and I was reflecting on the last couple of days, thinking how wonderful and amazing my God is. I mean this is no breaking the boundaries here but God is so willing to use me, even when most of the time, I only do half a job. Yet whilst I'm in training I can be used as far as my faith will take me. Just need to increase my faith. Also could see the pattern of as soon as the person finds out you are a Christian they seem to swear more and try and shock and almost insult your faith. Fortunately, my natural instinct is not to rise to it, but funny how people feel a need for protection...

Paul Knowlson

GO ... BUT WILL WE COME BACK?

Seek His Presence and Seek the Poor is the passion that fires our journey - the imperatives which burn. His presence is no small thing. The Holy Spirit is the Spirit of Jesus the presence of God within us, and overshadowing us. This is strong stuff provoking strong reaction, strong emotion- there is conviction of sin, of righteousness and judgement; explosive healing power; outrageous sacrifice and love carried in breathed on dust.

Sometimes He asks us to do more out of the ordinary things!

CONNEC T - DO EXTREME

Set out for at least one night, two days, taking these verses from Luke 9:3-6 at face value and see what happens - go with someone else and consult with others before you go!

"He told them take nothing for the journey - no staff, no bag, no bread, no money, no extra tunic. Whatever house you enter, stay there until you leave that town. If people do not welcome you, shake the dust of your feet when you leave their town, as a testimony against them." So they set out and went from village to village, preaching the gospel and healing people everywhere."

You can do it!

Does it take sandals? (hope not!)

NOW

" So what is the call? To be stateless, rootless, internationalist, owing no particular allegiance to anyone country or culture? Willing to give up all from family to material comforts to life itself for the cause? For God-fearing nomads, gypsy missionaries, spies and secret agents who can cross frontiers in the dark of night, change identities at the drop of a hat, sleep in a palace and a pigsty, and converse with both king and commoner? Is that what we are talking about is that achievable? Is it desirable? Is it necessary? It is the gospel I am afraid!" [10]

THE VISION

"The Vision is Jesus - obsessively, dangerously, undeniably Jesus. The vision is an army of young people...They are mobile like the wind, they belong to the nations. They need no passport... People write their addresses in pencil and wonder at their strange existence. They are free yet slaves to hurting and dirty and dying." [11] Pete Greig

Is He raising up a people movement of those who will go with no expectation of coming back; those who will find fresh expressions of team and sacrifice in this twenty-first century world; those who will go and root themselves, live and die in one place? Others whose lives will be apostolic journey, connecting deeply yet moving on. What might it look like if the fire carriers, the wild wanderers were released?

BLOG - LIVING ON A ONE-WAY TICKET'

"WHAT IF IT MEANS BEING POWERLESS, NOT IN CONTROL? WHAT IF IT MEANS BEING BOUND, TAKEN WHERE I DO NOT WANT TO GO AND KNOWING IT MAY LEAD TO DEATH?"

My life is not my own, to do with as I please, forgive me for ever thinking it was!

Paul set his face toward Rome, knowing that it would lead to prison. Agabus had prophesied over him - tying his hands and feet with a belt to show what lay ahead. Undeterred, he went saying, 'the will of the Lord be done.' No wonder he could write, 'for me to live is Christ, to die is gain.'
Is it?!!
What if I am kidnapped and beheaded by Hamas, Al-Quaeda, or assaulted by rebel soldiers. Why do I want to go to nations in crisis? Am I just a dreamer, an idealist? Sounds noble but what is real? What am I living for?
Look at Peter - standing on the shore, restored as a disciple only to be told by his most faithful friend, Jesus - Get over your identity crisis! Stop comparing yourself with your

brothers. Just be sure of this! 'When you were younger you girded yourself and walked where you wished; but when you are old, you will stretch out your hands and another will gird you and carry you where you do not wish to go' John 21:19. I don't think Jesus was talking about a 'care home' where Peter would see out his life!! He was martyred in Rome around AD 64 under the persecutions of Nero. Hmmm! Let's ponder on that!

Powerlessness - ultimate yieldedness of my future, my ability and strengths - empty-handed and empty-hearted. In my complete blindness to any sense of future, I choose to stand in agreement with His processes in this dark place. If my utter powerlessness can become a home I live from, then can His powerfulness flood through without resistance, not robbed by my agenda?

If signs and wonders do not accompany me from this place, then it seems untenable. What does it mean for my life to be a platform for His glory? So often I have striven for platform, being seen, being known, being heard - and for what profit??? In retrospect I can see NONE. Kill this soulishness in me - deal a mortal blow to my flesh - bind me to Your heart with fire.

Standing in a gap isn't enough - surely we must LIVE there, being a bridge so others can find their way home to the Father through a life laid down. Esther won a beauty competition, marrying a foreign king who governed her people. Suddenly she realised her success wasn't

for herself, she was positioned for her people. Now it's serious - 'If I perish, I perish' - For such a time as this. Aren't we in that day? For such a time as this? If not us - then who? If not now then when? - Life on a one-way ticket...

Anon

Plunge into His promise and emerge go on a martyrdom journey, no returning, no control on outcome, only yielding - Get a life? Get a death?

"I am always moving from the day of birth to the day of death...Christians must travel in perpetual pilgrimage as guests of the world".[13]
Columbanus

"Therefore let us concern ourselves with heavenly things and not human ones, and like pilgrims always sigh for our homeland, long for our homeland...Don't let us love the road more than the land to which it leads, lest we lose our homeland altogether. For we have such a homeland that we ought to love it".[14]
Columbanus

"In imagining the life of this sort of visionary vagabond we may already get a glimpse also of the practical side of that asceticism which puzzles those who think themselves practical. A man had to be thin to pass always out of the bars and out of the cage; he had to travel light in order to ride so fast and so far. It was the whole calculation , so to speak, of that innocent cunning, that the world was to be outflanked and outwitted by him. You could not threaten to starve a man who was ever striving to fast. You could not ruin him and reduce him to beggary, for he was already a beggar. There was lukewarm satisfaction in beating him with a stick, when he only indulged in little leaps and cries of joy because indignity was his only dignity. You could not put his head in a halter without the risk of putting it in a halo". [16]

SUNDAR SINGH

Sundar Singh was born in Rampur, a village in the Punjab on September 3,1889. He was educated at a missionary school and came to faith in 1905. His family threw him out of the house and disinherited him. Just over a month after his baptism he started his lifelong pilgrimage, a lifestyle of journey and selfless devotion, preaching the gospel with a simple sincerity that affected thousands of people.

"I will never forget the night I was driven out of my home. I slept outdoors under a tree, and the weather was cold. I had never experienced such a thing. I thought to myself: "Yesterday I lived in comfort. Now I am shivering, and I am hungry and thirsty. Yesterday I had everything I needed and more; today I have no shelter, no warm clothes, no food". Outwardly the night was difficult, but I possessed a wonderful joy and peace in my heart. I was following in the footsteps of my new master - of Yesu, who had nowhere to lay his head, but was despised and rejected. In the luxuries and comforts of home I had not found peace. But the presence of the Master changed my suffering into peace, and this peace has never left me". [15]

He was so impacted by the mystical experience that led to his conversion that he was always ready to talk about how Jesus had transformed his life. It was this conviction that Yesu was the Truth and that the deepest human needs and desires for peace were met in Him that fuelled his pilgrimage across many countries, travelling across India, Tibet and Nepal. Whilst on his journeys into Tibet, around 1912, he was attacked by violent fanatics. He was also arrested, thrown into a dry well and was left to die but for the intervention of a mysterious stranger. No-one knows quite where or how he died or even if he was taken like Enoch!

New age travellers provoke us to action through their wandering. I was challenged by the extremity of a man who sacrificed and focused his life to follow a dark vision he had received, it was a quest for hidden knowledge and spiritual power which over time became a prison. The vision and his spirit guides compelled him and took him to different nations, trapped him in a depth of demonic encounter. He later became a Christian overwhelmed by the simplicity of the love of Jesus.

Will we allow the incredible vision of Jesus to compel us, to draw us into a fresh abandonment to Him and His purposes? It will be worked out differently in our day but the call to adventure, to Wild Wandering is still being sounded.

SCUM-BAG APOSTLES

It seems to me that God has put us who bear His Message on stage in a theatre in which no-one wants to buy a ticket. We're something that everyone stands around and stares at, like an accident in the street. We're the Messiah's misfits. You might be sure of yourselves but we live in the midst of frailties and uncertainties. You might be well-thought-of by others, but we're mostly kicked around. Much of the time we don't have enough to eat, we wear patched and threadbare clothes, we get doors slammed in our faces, and we pick up odd jobs anywhere we can to eke out a living. When they call us names we say, "God bless you". When they spread rumours about us, we put in a good word for them. We're treated like garbage, potato peelings from the culture's kitchen. And it's not getting any better...we carry this precious message around in the unadorned clay pots of our ordinary lives. That's to prevent anyone from confusing God's incomparable power with us. As it is there's not much chance of that. You know for yourselves that we are not that much to look at...What they did to Jesus, they do to us - trial and torture, mockery and murder; what Jesus did among them, He does in us - He lives! Our lives are at constant risk for Jesus' sake, which makes Jesus' life all the more evident in us!"[17]

CONNECT - FOR A TIME

Set off on a Wild Wander, let Him lead you, let the fire in your eyes be a passion for His presence and a passion for the poor - go for as long as you can.

CONNECT - FOR LIFE

Set off on a Wild Wander, let Him lead you, let the fire in your eyes be a passion for His presence and a passion for the poor - go for a lifetime.

KEYS OF HEAVEN'S SIGHT >
KINGDOM BREAKOUT

KEYS OF HEAVEN'S SIGHT > KINGDOM BREAKOUT

Can we ask for more then we have dared to imagine, can we believe that what we have read in the Bible is available for us today? The vast depths of the sea are the most unexplored frontier on earth, containing half of all the living creatures on planet earth, yet it is dark and unknown.  As Christians there are unexplored realms in the supernatural full of His light and His glory that we are encouraged to step into, not for cheap thrills but out of a desire for intimacy and the unfolding of His Kingdom. There is a human yearning to explore the unknown, yet space is not the final frontier. We have been blind to other dimensions that are as real as air.

Sometimes we see into the spiritual realm with our natural eyes - when I have it has come as a bit of a shock! Yet, we mostly see into the spiritual realm with the 'eyes of our heart' and what we see is supernaturally natural and outrageously stunning.

Elisha had annoyed the King of Aram, who was at war with Israel, by his prophetic revelation into the king's battle plans. The king sent an army to capture him. Gehazi, Elisha's servant, saw the army and was terrified."Don't be afraid", the prophet answered, "Those who are with us are more than those who are with them". And Elisha prayed, "O Lord open his eyes so that he might see". Then the Lord opened the servant's eyes, and he looked and saw the hills full of horses and chariots of fire all round Elisha".We too need our spiritual senses to be awakened, our spiritual eyes to be opened (2Kings 6:16,17).

CONNECT WITH THE BIBLE

Pray these Ephesians verses regularly for yourself and others particularly that the "eyes of your heart may be enlightened". In fact the whole prayer is fantastic-

Ephesians 1:17-19a " I keep asking that the God of our Lord Jesus Christ, the glorious Father may give you the Spirit of wisdom and revelation, so that you may know him better. I pray also that the eyes of your heart may be enlightened in order that you may know the hope to which he has called you, the riches of his glorious inheritance in the saint, and his incomparably great power for us who believe..."

CONNECT WITH WONDER

The most wonderful thing about spiritual sight is looking at Jesus. We have been given in our hearts "the light of the knowledge of the glory of God in the face of Christ". (2 Cor 4:6). This takes us beyond words, yet even more amazingly as we behold the Lord's glory (2 Cor 3: 18) we are "transformed into his likeness with ever - increasing glory which comes from the Lord, who is the spirit".

He wants to give us a fresh sense of wonder. Ask Him to do that for you and to awaken a capacity to be awestruck, astounded, dazzled, lost in amazement, silenced, transfixed, unable to believe your eyes, lost in wonder! Thankfulness and gratitude open a door to wonder. Ask Him how He would like to develop that in you.

Make time to play, childlikeness and trust open a door to wonder. If you don't know how, ask Him what it means for you.

PHIL AND SARAH'S BLOG

We walked on to Swansea beach and found ourselves suddenly and unexpectedly surrounded by the presence of God and aware of angels standing on the shoreline. As we began to walk we noticed a strange pool in the sand with a stream going out of it into the sea. We looked into the pool and it looked like the water was coming up from an underground source, like a miniature geyser. It was the strangest thing either of us had seen on a beach and it was transfixing to look at.

We carried on along the beach just enjoying the presence of God. We looked at the sky and noticed that a small cloud in front of the sun was a golden colour, which stood out because all the other clouds were grey. The presence of God seemed to increase and as we looked at the sun again we saw fragments of a rainbow start to appear around the sun. One of us blurted, "It looks like Jesus"! and as we began to wonder what we were actually looking at, the sun and the rainbow cloud faded in front of our eyes! We looked across to the other side of the bay and saw that the sun was, in fact, on the other side of the sky.

These were signs to wonder at, a sign in the sky within a two week time frame following a major prophetic word. The pool may be a sign of the overflowing of ancient wells and springs. What we saw could have come straight out of Revelation 10:1-6

"Then I saw another angel coming down from heaven. He was robed in a cloud, with a rainbow above his head, his face was like the sun and his legs were like fiery pillars. He was holding a little scroll, which lay open in his hand. He planted his right foot on the sea and his left foot on the land, and he gave a loud shout like the roar of a lion. When he shouted the voices of the seven thunders spoke... THERE WILL BE NO MORE DELAY".

We are still wondering.

MEETING PLACE OF THE HEART

Intimacy is the key to encounter and the 'meeting place of the heart' is an amazing venue. Jesus wants to make his home there and we can chose to spend time there with him. In Revelation 3:20, Jesus is standing at the door and knocking, wanting a welcome, a response - which leads to this - "I will come in and eat with him and he with Me". Our hearts become his home, a place to linger, a place of conversation and revelation.

SOAKING

Soaking as has already been mentioned is a door to intimacy with Jesus, it is a door to the meeting place of the heart. It is also a place to receive deep healing and revelation of the Father Heart of God. It can be an environment in which He will take us into new realms in the supernatural in visions, trances, Third Heaven experiences, being translated in the Spirit, angelic encounters and more. He doesn't want us to be prescriptive but we can yield to him and to whatever He might want to show us or do.

Soaking is one emphasis that has come out of the Holy Spirit visitation in Toronto in January 1994. When this move of the Holy Spirit broke out at the same time in many places there was offence taken at the wildness of the manifestations.

Yet the ongoing fruit of the 'Toronto Blessing' is amazing. For many it brought healing, a fresh revelation of the Father heart of God, and a deep sense that He wants His church back. Many minds were offended (including mine!). This led to an exposing of our hearts, and if we yielded to Him, a greater release of the Holy Spirit in our lives. This includes miracles, signs and wonders born out of the intimacy of His presence.

In this ongoing move of the Spirit a true "Wildness" is released to follow Him and in embracing the first commandment He gives us greater capacity to embrace the second - to see the poor, the lost and the broken come home to the Father.

He is still at work and as He draws us we grow more confident that the Father's ability to keep and bless us is greater than the enemies power to deceive.

> # There are signs of a move of God, soaking is a major key to this breakout.

JUSTIN'S BLOG

Stop the clocks! Check this out! This week we had a major encounter with God. Dave, Rachel and myself had been soaking with Holy Spirit. It was refreshing. Rachel went up to bed at 11:00pm. At 11:05pm I was in the middle of talking to Dave about my desire for a 'spiritual baby' and I heard a roaring sound in my mind and whack! God came with extraordinary power. For 20 minutes it was intense heavy manifest presence of God. The wave ended and we looked at each other in wonder. Then the roaring sound came again and another stronger wave broke in on us. It was awesome! This went on over and over until is ended at 1:20am. During this time the room felt full of angels and glory. As one time I stopped even thinking. I was in a place of complete rest and connection with Jesus. It was warm and bright. It was like Jesus was standing in front of me. There were also times where I felt awe and fear of God. I hid behind the cushions. God said "The secret of the Lord is for those who fear Him". It was a time of encounter and revelation. I heard the Lord say "I have glorified my Name and I will glorify it again"! His voice was strong and deep. It was fearful! The Holy Spirit's presence was intense and deep pressing in on us. The room seemed to be buzzing. There was whizzing sound and it seemed like there were flying angels, thunder and glory. I believe we encountered the moving throne of Ezekiel 1. I heard a conversation from heaven repeated twice. There were four people or maybe angels - the first voice said "They're starting to believe"! The next one said "They're coming up here"! Another said, "It's so exciting"! The final voice said something like, "They have no idea what's going to hit them"! They were joyful and excited. I kept hearing the sound of laughter and talking it was like a crowd of children. I think there must be a party or great excitement in heaven. This encounter amazed us. It was like the Holy Spirit was showing us a side of Himself we had not seen before. I felt He was saying "This is what I'm like - I want to show the real Me"! He was disclosing Himself to us. His presence was penetrating and heavy. As one time my body felt like pulling out of this - but I decided that I wanted God more than the need for comfort - let the flesh die! My words don't do this justice! I felt the Lord say He wanted us to become accustomed to this realm. God so wants to reveal Himself in these days. Dave believes this is the revival Spirit manifesting. We both saw lightning at the same time - it was wild! I am so honoured by this encounter! No one can take it away from me - it's mine! His glory is amazing!

Justin Abraham

DO WE WANT THE ANGELS?

All this stuff about the supernatural realms raises a question - do we want the angels or are we too afraid of worshipping them to welcome them? It is easy to be dismissive of the angelic despite the interweaving of angelic messengers, angelic encounters and angelic help throughout scripture. If someone says they have seen an angel in a meeting it tends to divert as there is a surreptitious 'eyes right' peering and strained expressions as we desperately don't want to be the only person not to have seen the angel!

Some of the difficulties come because we find it harder to trust our own, and other peoples seeing with their 'spiritual eyes ' than our natural eyes. Our youngest son was having angelic encounters in the midst of being a cheeky, unwashed (unless pressured) eight year old, and was praying for me without much success that I would also, (that is see angels, not be unwashed!) In the end I did but only after I had repented of my fear, cynicism and unbelief over the whole thing. It was as if I found it harder to give room to the angelic than to miracles.

It seems that there is an increasing amount of angelic activity. Or maybe we have become more aware or more desperate in asking that the Lord would release the angels to help, and war on behalf of His people and on behalf of those who do not yet know Him.

This is the story of a sixteen year old I know and trust:

She was woken in the night by a strong sense of the presence of God, that increased and increased. She felt Jesus say to her that she was to go to Moriah chapel (where the 1904 revival broke out in Wales) stand outside and yell "Wake up". The chapel is just down the road from the college she goes to.

The next day she went and did what she had been asked. The first "Wake Up" was, understandably quiet! As she yelled more loudly the next time, she heard a loud yawning noise and saw that it was coming from a huge angel standing outside the chapel. The angel said to her "I have been asleep for a 100 years but the cry for revival in the land has now woken me up". The Angel started walking down the street...

In a large evangelistic meeting in a town known for prostitution in Andre Pradesh, India, I saw angels with my physical eyes above the open area the meeting was being held in. It was as if they were forming a canopy over the field. They came down closer during the time a call for salvation and healing was given. Many people came to faith and it was a night where the blind saw, the lame walked and a woman with a flow of blood (going against all her cultural norms) shared how Jesus had healed her.

There is so much more to embrace. There are growing numbers of contemporary angelic encounters. Some of them can be very practical or more "out there". Mark and I were driving a truck on a mission trip and got it jammed in a small Spanish street. The only way out was through a lane blocked by a large red car. A 'man' picked up the back of the car and wheeled the car as if it were a wheelbarrow round the corner, then disappeared - man/angel - you decide!

139

STUART'S BULGARIA BLOG

Whilst on a recent trip to Bulgaria and Romania I had a series of powerful encounters with God. At times the presence of God was so strong that we could barely stand or drive the car. God's presence came in waves that grew stronger each time. The angelic realm was so real. We were often aware of angels with us, even running along the side of the car as we travelled. I was woken up at 4.20am each morning with a strong sense of the presence of God. Bright lights and wave after wave of the glory of God filled my room, many times stopping me from being able to get up from my bed.

During one such time I felt myself being translated in the Spirit back to Llanelli. I found myself in a meeting which I later found out did take place. Also during this encounter I prayed for a lady who is now well. One afternoon during a meal time I was again taken back to Llanelli in the spirit and prayed for someone.

The awareness of God was so strong even a lady serving us in a petrol station was powerfully touched by the Holy Spirit. Everywhere we went the presence of God would impact people's lives, causing them to laugh, cry or fall down. During our time in Romania, a young girl 14 years old was so touched by God in every meeting that even as she came into the room the presence of God would come on her. By the end of the week she was filled with God and His glory. Going to school a few days later she noticed a girl who was regularly nasty to her. As this girl came near her the power and presence of God fell on her. The girl began laughing, as did the whole class as God's presence came on them all. Ever since that day there has been a great change and the girls are now best friends. The girl and her family are seeing an on-going move of the Holy Spirit in their home.   Stuart Watkins

CONNECT - ENCOUNTERS OF A SPIRITUAL KIND...

Is it ok to have spiritual experiences? - Yes - the Bible is full of them.

How do we check that we are not totally "off it"?
- CHECK WITH THE BIBLE;
- CHECK WITH TRUSTWORTHY CHRISTIANS;
- ASK YOURSELF HOW IT HAS IMPACTED YOU - ARE YOU AT PEACE?
- CHECK OUT THE FRUIT IT IS PRODUCING/ HAS PRODUCED.

This is not anything like an exhaustive list just an appetiser! Study, meditate on these things-
- Hearing the audible voice of God - Isaiah 30:21
- Being led by the Spirit - Luke 2:25-27
- Visions come in many forms - Acts 9:10-15
- Trances - Acts 10:9-16
- Angelic visitations - Hebrews:13:2
- Dreams - Matthew 2:12
- Visitation of Jesus - Acts 9: 4-6
- Transported in the Spirit - Acts 8;39
- Translated in the Spirit - 2 Cor 12:2-5

Spend time soaking in His presence and see what happens

BLOG - ENCOUNTERS WITH GOD

Sometimes an encounter can shape the course of our lives -

Wednesday November 17th, 1999
Today when praying on retreat with others for Wales went into a new place in God. I was in the Spirit and with Jesus walking up to a latched gate. Jesus was playful, I was a bit scared to go through although I did, into a beautiful green place. Jesus, abandoned, young, vigorous, playing with me, swinging me round, shaking out religion and false responsibility.

I kept saying, "You can't, You can't do this. You can't be like this". He was exuberant, playing, wild... I asked, "Lord, what does this mean for Wales?" He said, "I AM RESTORING THE CHILDHOOD OF THE NATION". Go with Him up a hill and see a large boulder poised on the top. Instinctively I know this huge boulder is shame and reproach and instinctively I knew what He was going to do -

I said, "You can't, You musn't".

He said, "YOU JUST WATCH ME!" He pushed it lightly and it crashed down the hill.

(Many months later I came back to that same place and saw green shoots emerging where the boulder had once been).

Thursday November 18th, 1999

On retreat still, when praying see the gate again. Jesus standing on the other side, I go through to be with Him. Suddenly aware my back is covered with scars and the shame of other deep unhealed wounds...It switches to Wales, the scars, the wounds on the back the contours and textures in the Welsh landscape. Other wounds hidden in the underbelly, deep in the earth.

"I am going to take you to the Father".

"You can't", shame and fear gripped me, felt too weak to walk.

"I will carry You". He took me towards what I knew to be the torn veil of His body, the spear hole in Jesus' side. Go through into a courtyard, flames of fire on each side and an overwhelming sense of the love of the Father, soft white light, incredible kindness, glory,... .torn between glory and the nation, glory, glory, glory - wounds forgotten - awe, "Only dared to come to ask You for my people... What do You see when you look at us"?

The light changed to gold, molten glory flowing out - I see glory as gold pouring out on the nation. I ask Him, "Evan saw 100,000 what do You see now"? He said, "A whole nation".

...strength, glory, glory, running to herald, torches setting oil wells on fire - "How can we run without Your glory and tell? How can we, without Your presence?... Can my friends come ... saw them covered in the gold of His glory. Baptised in fire as we waited before Him...

"What is the message we run with"? - "My presence and the poor. My glory flowing to the places of least resistance... You will find the poor amongst the rich and the rich amongst the poor".

Saw Wales, alongside other nations that will fully turn as a small stone in the Bride's engagement ring - a token given before time. Then suddenly taken down into Second Heaven and see filthy wells pumping dark pollution into the atmosphere, shutting down as they are encircled with light...A covering of unending song, prayer and worship rising over the land - that the harvest could come safely in. Apostolic teams flowing across the land covered in His glory, flowing in and out coming back to the tent of His presence...

This has gripped me, shaped my journey these last years - "A whole nation" - "His presence and the poor" - I can't unsee it.

"I am coming for the nation, glory flowing like molten gold to the people and places of least resistance, teams flowing, running - the message - My presence and the poor. A nation transformed for the transforming of other nations".

GO DEEPER - ADVENTURES IN THE HEAVENLY REALM

"But God, who is rich in mercy, because of His great love with which He loved us, even when we were dead in trespasses, made us alive together with Christ (by grace you have been saved), and raised us up together, and made us sit together in the heavenly places in Christ Jesus, that in the ages to come He might show the exceeding riches of His grace in His kindness toward us in Christ Jesus" (Ephesians 2:4-7).

Who was it that caused us to think that adventures in the heavenly realm do not belong to the 'normal Christian'? According to Paul not only is the door to these realms wide open for us, it is meant to be our normal dwelling place. Read these verses again:

- 'But God', before this verse we see our normal expectation would be that of being 'dead in trespasses and sins' (2:1) But God steps in;
- 'who is rich in mercy because of His great love with which He loved us,' cannot hold back from acting on our behalf, with an astonishing purpose.
- 'even when we were dead in trespasses, made us alive together with Christ' - part one, He transfers us from death to life by His grace, we are included in Christ's resurrection. By grace we are saved, Hallelujah!
- 'and raised us up together' - there's more. In a corporate sense we are all then raised up, not only from the dead but to another realm.
- 'and made us sit together in the heavenly places in Christ Jesus' - not an add-on afterthought for the super spiritual, but what God has done for us. We ARE sat together with Christ in the heavenly places. What we need is a revelation of the truth of this and what it means for us in our walk with Him on the earth. This is not a future truth, but a present truth that Paul prays that the eyes of our hearts and understanding be opened to grasp (1:17-23).
- 'in the ages to come He might show' - this is not a passing interest but of eternal importance. God is putting something in place as a proof, a declaration, a show
- 'the exceeding riches of His grace in His kindness toward us in Christ Jesus' - all of the preceeding is an outflow of God's kindness expressed towards US - yes that includes all who are IN CHRIST.

One of the first accounts of an heavenly adventure is that of Jacob fleeing his brother Esau's deadly intentions, seeing heaven opened above him with angels ascending and descending to and from heaven Genesis 28.

Under the old covenant, the people of God had Moses and then the priesthood to stand between them and God. Exodus 20:18-21 describes how they in fear 'stood afar off', boundaries having been set lest they approach God and die (19:12), whilst Moses drew near to the thick darkness where God was. When he descended the mountain his face so shone with the reflected Glory of God that he covered it with a veil lest they notice the glory depart.

Yet even under this once removed relationship with God, we hear of the exceptions who catch a glimpse of the Glory. Moses' experience with the burning bush, Sinai and the Tent of Meeting all speak of heaven breaking into earth. Ezekiel (chapters 1-3,8-11, 37, 40-48) and Daniel (chapters 7-12) both have astonishing experiences of the heavenly realms.

Daniel describes dreams and visions in which sees the Ancient of Days enthroned, and the broad sweep of history is set out before him, the rise and fall of empires and the coming never ending Kingdom of God.

Ezekiel experiences adventures in the Spirit in which he is uncertain sometimes whether he is physically transported or is seeing things in a vision they are so real and immediate. To the western mind they seem fantastical, and our inclination is to allegorise and look for the truth behind the experience. But the Lord's ways are so much higher than ours (Isaiah 55:8-9), indeed past finding out (Job 9:10, Romans 11:33). Who are we to seek to put boundaries on what He can and cannot do!! In the uncomfortable balance between God's unsearchable wisdom and ways, and my limited understanding, there is only one place the shift must occur. "If any man lacks wisdom, let him ask of God" (James 1:5), such truth can only be received by God revealing it to us, and by us so hearing the word of Christ that faith for it is born in us (Romans 10:17).

Things changed when Immanuel was born, God with us, revealing the Father to us. He made His dwelling among us. Now, according to our witness John, we can behold His glory as the only Son coming from the Father full of grace and truth (John 1).

Hebrews 4:14-16 and 10:19-22, speak of a boldness in our approaching the throne of God, by a new and living way opened up for us in Jesus by His body broken and blood poured out. Let us so approach Him and be open to all that He chooses to reveal of Himself to us.

The Bible closes with the supreme adventure in the heavenlies in the book of Revelation. The first chapter of which provides a safeguard for all that would dare to venture into such realms. The vision here of the Risen Ascended Lord is so awesome as to render John as dead. True encounters at this level will always bring a heightened awe for God and His holiness.

Yet whether we experience such open heaven visions or not, the truth of our sitting in the heavenlies together with Christ must be part of our lived-out faith. We need to ask for this perspective in our prayer life, that we see earth from heaven down, not just from our earthly position. Then we can begin to truly pray 'Your kingdom come Your will be done on earth as we see it in heaven.' We can begin to call more powerfully and with revealed understanding for an aligning of earth with heaven on specific matters. Things bound on earth can more fully be bound in heaven, those loosed on earth loosed in heaven (Matthew 16:19, 18:18-20).

Being less earthbound in our thinking will open our lives more fully to the Spirit of truth to guide us into all truth (John 16:13).

Hywel Rhys Edwards

"YOUR KINGDOM COME...'

"Your Kingdom come, your will be done on earth as it is in heaven" (Matt 6: 10). We are called to be Kingdom people, demonstrating His Kingdom and bringing in His Kingdom here on earth. It will often lead to a Kingdom clash. Jesus said "If I cast out demons by the Spirit of God surely the Kingdom of God has come upon you". It may be messy, confrontational, certainly full of laughter. The Kingdom is what happens when heaven comes to earth. Heaven on earth means no sorrow, or sickness, or pain.

When the Kingdom breaks through and earth lines up with heaven there are healings and miracles, signs and wonders. Jesus announced His Kingdom manifesto in His home town of Nazareth His manifesto is ours also, to be declared and demonstrated in His authority in every place we walk.

God's Spirit is on me,
He's chosen me to preach the Message of good news to the poor,
Sent me to announce pardon to prisoners and recovery of sight to the blind,
To set the burdened and battered free,
To announce, "This is God's year to act".
(The Message Luke 4:18,19)

GO DEEPER - THE KINGDOM

"The Gospel is the good news of the Kingdom involving a whole new way of relating to God, one another and the world, encountered by revelation on the basis of repentance and faith. It was initiated and demonstrated by the incarnation of Jesus and secured and established by His death and resurrection. To receive it is to be immediately part of the church, which exists as a witness to the revelation, a school of discipleship, a spiritual army against the devil, and Christ's agent to unlock the Kingdom of God on earth. Writing in the book of Acts, Luke describes the essentials of how the early church worked this out: "And they were continually devoting themselves to the apostles' teaching and to fellowship, to the breaking of bread and to prayer" (Acts 2:42).

These ingredients of church life were and are the key to having favour with the people and daily church growth. They are the essential means whereby the fire of the Kingdom spreads. When these expressions of gospel Christianity have been flourishing in Europe, the Kingdom of God has been strong. Where they have been extinguished or weakened so has the Kingdom of God". [1]

Jesus walked without sin and in deep connection with His Father, dependant on the Holy Spirit. He said (John 5:19) "the Son can do nothing by himself; he can only do what he sees the Father doing". Jesus walked in a deep compassion, miracles demonstrating Kingdom reality to a desperate people. If we claim to 'live in Him' we must 'walk as Jesus did' (1 John 1: 6). This means a walk of yielded strength, a learnt dependence and MIRACLES. Every time we risk and reach out to someone and pray for their healing; command the sickness to go, the Kingdom has come. Compassion, His kindness, compels us.

What if they are not instantly healed, do not receive the miracle they wanted? At the very least there will have been a taste of the kindness of heaven, the fact that someone cared enough to really see them, to spend time with them and to stand with them in the things we do not understand. The more miracles we experience - the lame walking, the blind seeing, the more we long to see. And the deeper the cry becomes for those who terminally ill, the mentally ill, the desperate, the demonized. Yet, he calls us to make the kingdom our way of life and every risk we take calls more of heaven to earth.

When we were told that our 6 week old daughter was mentally handicapped it devastated us, confirming what we had instinctively known. When we prayed for her that night (in the midst of a nappy change!) her floppy unresponsive body and her dead eyes received a miracle and for the very first time she smiled and as she did it was as if a light went on - connections that hadn't been there spontaneously formed.

Her first smile is still the most beautiful thing I have ever seen. I don't know why she was healed and why the mentally handicapped children I had previously worked with and prayed for hadn't been. There is much we don't understand but what I know is that we must see the place of overshadowing, of encounter with Him brought down from the mountain top and on to the street.

Jesus came down from the mountain where Peter, James and John saw Him overshadowed in glory to see the other disciples failing in their attempt to cast a demon out of a tormented boy racked with seizures. Jesus cast the demon out and later explained to the disciples why they hadn't seen it shift.

" Because you have so little faith, I tell you the truth, if you have faith as small as a mustard seed, you can say to this mountain. 'Move from here to there' and it will move. Nothing will be impossible to you" (Matthew 17:20).

The mountain, the place of the revelation of His glory, can be transferred to the street, and He says it doesn't take much faith to see it shift. Perhaps the more we experience of His overshadowing in times alone with Him the more confident we become to move in the authority we have in him on the street, in our homes and work-places.

The territory of signs, wonders, healings, and miracles is a huge one to explore and full of giants; but we can't back off. The post-modern culture connects easily with spiritual experiences, healings and miracles open the doors to people's hearts like nothing else. This is a time for power encounters and if we let Him, He would like to train us. The biggest hindrance can be the inconvenience, we are to busy with other things! If these are to be days of 'Kingdom come' we need to pursue it diligently - it could be the biggest adventure of our lives.

There are 'healing pools' opening up in different locations, Bethesda places as in John 5 where the angels turn up. There are also the John 9 moments where Jesus meets a blind man on the street and sends him to the pool of Siloam (sent) to wash the spit sandwich off his eye. There are pools and rivers of healing being released and we can flow with both; the ones who don't come to the pool can be found on the street and can themselves be sent out as a witness of the King and his Kingdom.

CONNECT- HE WOULD LIKE TO TRAIN US, WILL WE LET HIM?.......

- What does it mean for Him to train us?
- Ask Him what this means for you? Does it look different from what you were expecting?
- How does He want to train you to move in signs and wonders?
- Ask Him how this will affect your life.

CONNECT WITH THE SPIRITUAL GIFTS HE WANTS TO GIVE YOU

- If you have not been baptised in the Holy Spirit ask Him to (Acts 10:44-47) is a help if you feel disqualified..
- He want to release the gifts of the Spirit to you (1 Cor 12:4-11). Word of wisdom, word of knowledge, gift of faith, gifts of healing, gifts of miracles, discerning of spirits, prophecy, tongues and interpretations of tongues. This may be something very new or very familiar. He wants to release a fresh expectancy as to what He wants to do. It is time to take risks.
- Each day for a week ask for opportunities to move in the gifts of the Spirit - you will be amazed.

He said to them, "Go into all the world and preach the good news to all creation. Whoever believes and is baptized will be saved, but whoever does not believe will be condemned. And these signs will accompany those who believe: in my name they will drive out demons; they will speak in new tongues; they will pick up snakes with their hands; and when they drink deadly poison, it will not hurt them at all; they will place their hands on sick people and they will get well" (Mark 16:15-18).

LETS' DO IT! Pray for opportunities then take them.

OPEN DOORS

The door to the wardrobe in 'The Lion the Witch and the Wardrobe' opened the way to an incredible world, different, yet strangely familiar. There are literal as well as spiritual doors that He wants to open to us.

Here are some of the doors that opened for Paul.

- Paul stayed on at Ephesus until Pentecost, "Because a great door for effective work has opened to me and there are many who oppose me" (1 Cor 16:9).

- Paul went to Troas to preach the gospel because, "The Lord had opened a door for me" (2 Cor 2:12).

- "And pray for us too that God may open a door for our message, so that we may proclaim the mystery of Christ for which I am in chains" (Col 4:3).

There are doors Jesus wants to open for us. Ask Him about the doors he wants to take you through and how He wants you to prepare for them. In Acts 9:36-43 we find the story of Dorcas "who was always doing good and helping the poor". She died and the widows were distraught because of her kindness and the way she had practically cared for them. Peter prayed for her, he didn't dare not to(!), and she was raised from the dead. The door was flung wide open -"this became known all over Joppa, and many people believed in the Lord".

Care for the poor opens the door to the miraculous; acts of kindness are accessible to all, to give and to receive. They are major door openers, as is simply doing your job. Rhoda a servant girl, was in work and opened the door to a miracle- Peter after his miraculous escape from prison (Acts 12:13,14).

Homes are frequently the place of miracles, healings and salvation. Lydia's conversion in Philippi led to the conversion of her whole household (Acts 16:14,15).

Homes, workplaces and streets seem to be favourite places for the opening of incredible doors of opportunity - it is Kingdom breakout on the streets and maybe even in the churches!

BLOG - CEFNCEAU

Myself and someone else on the team had a sense before we went out that God was saying look for open doors. When we reached the estate, we took that literally when we saw an open door and went up to the house and ended up praying for a lady whose 2 year old son had potential brain damage. Then we carried on and saw another open door and prayed for this woman who had just recently divorced and had moved to the estate, but was finding it hard to settle there. Then we carried on walking around and saw an open window this time, and a woman standing there looking at us, probably wondering what on earth we were doing. We stopped, waved nervously, and she waved back, also nervously and then she came to the door and opened it. We found out that she used to come to the youth club at Antioch Church, Llanelli, a few years ago, but had since fallen away from God. We prayed for her and knew that it was a real divine appointment.

Zoe Britnell

Words of knowledge and visions can be a door

BLOG - BLAENAU FFESTINIOG

Before we went out on the streets of Blaenau we prayed for words of knowledge and I had one about a woman with athritis in her right arm. The first person we went up to on the high street was a woman with athritis in her right arm and when we told her that we knew God was going to lead us to someone with that, her faith levels went up. She wanted prayer and whilst praying for her, we could see the Holy Spirit was really on her as she was shaking and nearly fell over in the street. We could really see the breakout of 'the river' of the Holy Spirit flowing through the streets of Blaenau and that God was specifically leading us to people that He wanted to touch that day.

He had shown me in a vision a woman he wanted us to meet in Blaenau- a New Ager with a stripy hat. When we did meet up I discovered she was a pagan, with a tender heart and a deep concern for her little girl. She was touched that the God she didn't believe in would reach out to her in this way. She wanted us to pray for her.

Zoe Britnell/Jen Hallet

Miracles and healings can be a door. You can see a healing pool form wherever you are.

BLOG - LLANELLI

Llanelli Town Centre - While we were going around Llanelli town centre we saw a man who was having difficulty walking. So we started to chat to him and asked him if he wanted us to pray for him. He said yes and we prayed for him to have more movement in his legs. Then we asked him to try to do something he had not done before. He started to walk and bend down on his legs. He said that he hadn't managed to do that in ages, and that they felt better. It seemed that Jesus healed him that day.

Also, while going into the indoor market in Llanelli, we saw a group of women sitting in the café area. We started to chat to them and asked if any wanted prayer. One woman said that she needed prayer for her athritis. Then suddenly, we were surrounded by people who wanted prayer. Another wanted prayer for athritis, another for epilepsy, another for cancer, and one woman wanted prayer because she was lonely as her husband had died two years ago. We prayed for them, and as we were about to go, the two women that had athritis told us that they could feel tingling and heat all up and down their bodies. God was really touching them, and it was like the overshadowing of the Holy Spirit in Acts 5, where the sick were brought out into the streets, as we were suddenly surrounded by people, desperate for prayer and the reality of Jesus.

Zoe Britnell

DAVE'S BLOG

THE DOOR OF SUPERNATURAL GLORY
OPENS FOR WALES

From the time I became a Christian in 1992 I believed in and longed for mystical Christianity. I refused to settle for average or mundane and believed that the God who translated Elijah and allowed Peter to walk on water was my God. The first life-changing vision I had was when I was in a friend's flat and suddenly the ceiling felt like fire and descended on me and for three hours I became a flaming fire as I beheld open-eyed visions of stadiums in Wales filled with people, I knew the same fire that was on me was on them and that it was Revival Fire. At that point I heard the voice of the Lord say, "My people must re-align their thoughts because I'm going to shake this nation". At that point the guy whose flat it was started shaking me and telling me I had to leave, I thought I had only been there five minutes until I looked at my watch and saw I'd really been there over three hours.

In 2005 I had two experiences that stirred my heart. I was driving my car one day and it started to snow (yes snow) inside my car. For about five minutes I was in a car that was being snowed into. A few weeks later I was on a plane and I watched with my physical eyes as a two foot square block of heavy rain descended inside the plane for about ten minutes. After these two encounters I asked God what was happening and he said to me that He had opened a door of Supernatural Glory over the nation. Since October of 2005 I have been experiencing the fruit of God opening this Door to the nation. This Door has opened a way to a whole new realm of supernatural life. Its not uncommon now for God's thick Glory to come and remain on me for hours at a time and recently for two days, where it became very difficult to function. This Door has also opened up a new highway for angels to come. Many nights I get woken up now with the room full of angels. Even this week I had another encounter where just like Jacob I wrestled with an angel for 30 minutes.

I think these things are so cool. More God! I encourage you to walk through the Door of Supernatural Glory and see where it takes you!

Dave Vaughan

HISTORY - PAST HEROES

SUPERNATURAL MONKS - ANGELS AND DEMONS

BRYNACH, was known for his angelic encounters on a mountain between Nevern and Newport. The mountain became known as Carn Ingli ('The Mountain of Angels').

He also sorted out some demons. Wild animals, and sometimes outlaws, lurked in the woods nearby and when he settled at the site now called Pontfaen in the Gwaun valley (in north Pembrokeshire), 'he freed that place from unclean spirits. They, roving about it every night, with dreadful outcries, and filling it with horrid howlings, rendered it uninhabitable till that day' [2]

St Patrick's Breastplate is an eighth century Irish hymn which may or may not have been written by Patrick - it is great whatever! And carries a graphic understanding of spiritual authority and warfare:

" I bind unto myself today
The strong name of the Trinity
By Invocation of the same
The Three in One and One in Three.
Christ be with me, Christ within me
Christ behind me, Christ before me,
Christ beside me, Christ to win me
Christ to comfort and restore me,
Christ beneath me, Christ above me,
Christ in quiet, Christ in danger,
Christ in hearts of all that love me,
Christ in mouth of friend or stranger
Against all Satan's spells and wiles,
Against all false words of heresy,
Against the knowledge that defies,
Against the heart's idolatry.
Against the wizards evil craft,
Against the death wound and the burning,
The choking wave , the poisoned shaft,
Protect me, Christ , till thy returning".

BEUNO was a holy man who probably died around the year 642. He is credited with raising six or seven people from the dead. He had a great reputation for giving huge feasts, apparently miraculously produced from next-to-nothing. [3]

BRENDAN too was known for perfuming every kind of miracle:

"After raising of dead men, healing lepers, blind, deaf, lame and all kinds of sick folk….after expelling demons and vices…..after performance of mighty works and miracles too numerous to mention, St Brendan drew near to the day of his death". [4]

LESSONS TO LEARN FROM THE LIFE OF SAMSON OF DOL

We have some good information about Samson from "The Life of St Samson of Dol". It was written, at the request of Bishop Tigernomal, Abbot of Dol, by a monk of Dol, probably between 610 and 615, only about fifty years after the death of Samson and when people who had known him would still have been alive.

Samson was one of the great missionary saints of the sixth century, born in South Wales, he was trained by St Illtyd. The greater part of his work was established through his travels in Cornwall and Brittany, these wanderings were characterised by power encounters and miracles. It was through these miracles that he saw the Kingdom come and the church established.

When he was travelling in North Eastern Cornwall through the Hundred of Trigg he came upon the chieftain Guedian and his people dancing in worship before an idol. They said they were simply re-enacting an old play but Samson forbade them to do it and confirmed his authority when a boy involved in the ritual fell from his horse and died. Samson then raised him from the dead - it took two hours of prayer. He persisted in prayer, not giving up when there wasn't a quick result. He also followed the pattern of Jesus and got them to back off so he could pray for the boy unhindered.

"For a certain boy, driving horses at full speed, fell from a swift horse to the ground, and twisting his head as he fell headlong, remained just as he was flung, little else than a lifeless corpse. Then St. Samson speaking to the tribesmen as they wept around the body, said, 'You see that your image is not able to give life to the dead man. But if you will promise that you will utterly destroy this idol and no longer adore it, I, with God's assistance, will bring the dead man to life.' And they consenting, he commanded them to withdraw a little further off, and, after praying earnestly over the lifeless man for two hours, he delivered him, who had been dead, alive and sound before them all. Seeing this, they all with one accord, along with the afore-mentioned chief, prostrated themselves at St. Samson's feet and utterly destroyed the idol. [Samson understood that it was a power encounter with the forces of darkness.] Then the far-sighted chief made them all come and ratify their allegiance by baptism at the hands of St. Samson".[5]

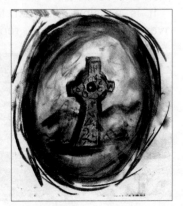

Samson followed this event by replacing the "abominable image" on the summit of a certain hill with the symbol of the Cross.

As soon as he landed in Brittany he saw a whole household transformed before travelling onto Dol where he founded the monastery named after him and with which he is most associated. Here is an account of his opening miracles in

Brittany where he sought an opening through a 'man of peace' and called for miracles that would open the region to Jesus:

"But, as they were landing from the ship, they saw a hut of no great size standing not far from the harbour, and as St. Samson drew near to it, he saw on the threshold of the little dwelling an individual making lamentation and ever gazing towards the sea. In fact St. Samson, directing his steps towards him, inquired of him the reason of this; the individual for his part said to him, 'It is now three days and as many nights since I waited in this harbour the coming of the helper from beyond the sea whom God promised me'. St. Samson said unto him, 'What is thy trouble?' He said, 'I have in this house a leprous wife, moreover, a demoniac daughter and I had the promise of their cure in this harbour'. St. Samson, to be sure, immediately entered within the house and pouring forth prayer over both of the sick women, with God's help delivered them safe and sound before them all. And, going forth from thence, having God for his guide, he discovered a most suitable spot in these parts and founded a famous monastery which to this day, by an appropriate use of language, is called Dol. From that place he planted the seed of many works of a wonderful character and founded many monasteries throughout almost the entire province, which if all of them were described, one by one, we should be led to exceed the task we undertook". [6]

His power encounters flowed from times of solitude and contemplation. His face was described as 'radiant, like that of an angel.'

There is much to learn if like Samson and Paul we will be able to see whole regions fully reached by the power of the gospel. "By the power of signs and miracles, through the power of the Spirit. So from Jerusalem all the way round to Illyricum, I have fully proclaimed the gospel of Christ. It has always been my ambition to preach the gospel where Christ was not known, so that I would not be building on someone else's foundation. Rather as it is written, 'Those who were not told about Him will see and those who have not heard will understand'" (Romans 15:19-21).

It is possible for vast territories to be overshadowed by the glory of God, Elohim, overshadows the earth, renews it in His creative power. As He spoke and life formed, so

can we, filled with the Holy Spirit speak His word and see creative miracles break out... eyeballs form, a new heart beat, a hand appear. There are creative miracles on every level in every sphere of life waiting to be released - WILL we hear Him, will we speak the word, take the risk? Will we take hold of the keys of heaven's sight and see the Kingdom Breakout?

SOUND AND LIGHT
COMMUNITY

SOUND AND LIGHT COMMUNITY

In these days authentic, real, honest, covenant, committed communities will be seen as a miracle. They will be seen as a sign and a wonder where we can learn how to connect, how to communicate, how to move through our pain to a deeper wholeness in Jesus and where it is safe to be as wild as He created us to be... those borne by the wind of His Spirit.

Community is the stepping-off point for wild adventures in God the safe place to come back to, the place where we are grounded in the reality of expressing our faith in the twenty-first century. It is also a wild adventure of its own which is counter-cultural, radical and a major act of spiritual warfare against the cult of the individual, self-protection, control and small-mindedness.

Community is a fundamental expression of a covenant-keeping God who has extended community into this world through His Son and by the power of the Holy Spirit working through the church. Community has never been optional, it is an essential part of the expression of the Kingdom of God breaking through into this world.

We live in a world still reeling from the emotional effects of two world wars, nuclear holocaust at Hiroshima and global terrorism. Emotional orphans abound where the ability to connect emotionally has been significantly affected. Fear and isolation are a major part of the enemy strategy towards self-destruction. We are surrounded by options to manage our pain - drugs, alcohol, work, shopping, sex. Psychologists are beginning to question the focus on counselling over the last forty years of the twentieth century as to whether the "deeper human needs are better met by simple human relationships of love, trust, care and accountability. It is the loss of those kinds of relationships which have produced the many neuroses and pathologies of western society". [1]

This world is not a safe place, we live in a fragmented and rapidly changing society, highly individualistic, rife with family breakdown, a world where it is not safe to show yourself, where to survive we blend in with the crowd - surfie, townie, mosher, goth, skater. A post-modern, post-Christian world with a multitude of values, a pick'n'mix mentality where experience equals truth and whatever works for me is good and god, whether that be crystals, woodland rites, nature worship, wicca or paganism. A world not too dissimilar to the one the early Celtic Christians encountered.

We are surrounded by examples of and attempts at community - family, marriage, friendship, TV soaps, interest groups, dance/club culture, alternative lifestyle communities,

156

reality TV, an endless variety. The challenge we face as twenty-first century Christians is to provide the world we live in with an authentic, viable and visible expression of community that works. But why do we find it so difficult? The predominant expression of church today is still fundamentally based on the 'Roman' model of centralised authority structures and control. There are attempts to 'de-construct' and to see what will emerge.

Philosopher Alasdair MacIntyre characterises contemporary society as a "collection of strangers", a "new Dark Ages" and suggests that during the demise of the Roman Empire it was small communities of virtue - monastic communities - which saved western civilisation from barbarity. He suggests further that it is small communities of virtue who will have the most powerful effect on our present society". [2]

These communities small and large provided the safe places, the launch pads, for the wild wanderings of many of the Celtic saints. In our day how do we build communities that answer the cry for connection from outside the walls of our churches and are also safe places from which to launch great ventures?

Deb Chapman

GO DEEPER WITH COMMUNITY

"If anyone loves me, he will obey my teaching. My Father will love him, and we will come to him and make our home with him" (John 14:23).

God is community, Father, Son and Holy Spirit, and we become part of Their community and demonstrate that community in our relationships with each other. Church is a community of people gathered to Jesus where there is a commitment to Jesus, to His word, to each other and the Holy Spirit is present amongst them. Community is a manifestation of the Holy Spirit.

In calling the twelve to Himself Jesus chose intentional community. He showed them how to work it out with each other, leaving them the new commandment to love each other in the same way that He had loved them. He modelled intentional community as a sending base from which they went on their own wild adventures, returning with joy as even the demons were subject to them.

TRUE COMMUNITY

There is a growing movement of those, particularly in their twenties, who want to live in a more radical way and are choosing to live amongst those on the margins of society, often choosing to live in community. It is a fresh expression of Celtic Christianity; a recapturing in new clothes of the upside-down life of St. Francis. This expressed in simple daily choices of obedience and kindness, a dying to preference and opinion, worked out in community and extended family.

We have lived in extended family for many years sometimes, but not always, with those from backgrounds of abuse and addiction. It has been joy and pain! We have mostly learnt how we would do it differently. One of our daughters, then age six, was crying and praying for someone on drugs who had just done a runner from the house.She then asked why "Kate" had gone back to smoking rugs? The visual image made us laugh in the midst of our loss!

We are designed for relationship and community and our brains are wired in such a way that connection with people whose faces "light up" when they see us builds "joy strength" in us. Where the development of joy has not been a part of childhood, our capacity to handle trauma and strong emotion is impaired. The challenge for any community is to provide a safe context to heal and grow. Part of this is to model healthy relationships and care-giving thus providing that which was lacking in early relationships. This aspect of community, alongside prayer ministry, is vital for our journey to wholeness but has historically been overlooked by many church contexts - maybe as too big a challenge, but it seems to be the way forward for those coming to faith in this generation.

To sustain a lifestyle of 'incarnating' Jesus amongst the poor the first commandment has to be the first commandment, "love the Lord your God with all your heart, mind and soul" or all you are left with is the dry dust of exhaustion. The focus of devotion and the rest which celebrates our humanity, the time for friendship and simply 'to be'- with no agenda, sometimes needs to happen outside the intense physical and spiritual environment in which we live. This is, or seems to be, a real challenge to outwork!

HOW DO WE DO COMMMUNITY?

As people we all have the ability to live community, but it is like hidden treasure, rough mineral buried in the earth, we have to dig for it, it needs working on and the process of continual cutting, sanding and polishing produces a precious gem.[3] Community has many facets, many sides, and not one aspect of it fully defines it.

The western expression of early Celtic Christians understood the dynamics of community. I believe this can point us in the right direction as we seek to find new ways of being communities of faith, connecting with each other and with those who don't yet know Him.

CONNECT - FULLY HUMAN?! HOLY LEISURE - WHAT'S THAT?

As well as times in His presence and living all that out in the day to day we need what the mad desert monks called "otium sanctum" - holy leisure. This means a life in balance, being at peace in the midst of the activites of the day. It means an ability to rest, to enjoy beauty and that it is ok to pace yourself. Burnout (as I have experienced it) is not a mark of being spiritual! Holy leisure means enjoying and having time to be fully human!

- Chew on this -
"Are you tired? Worn out? Burned out on religion? Come to me. Get away with me and you'll recover your life . I'll show you how to take a real rest. Walk with me and work with me - watch how I do it. Learn the unforced rhythms of grace. I won't lay anything heavy or ill-fitting on you. Keep company with me and you'll learn to live freely and lightly" (The Message, Matt 11: 28-29).

- Ask Him what holy leisure means for you.

- Ask Him to help you learn more of the "unforced rhythms of grace".

Two key elements for the early Celtic Christians were -

- Non-hierarchical leadership

Leadership in the monastic communities was traditionally by the Abbot or Abbess meaning father or mother. They were not based on the hierarchy of a military order but functioned more like an extended family, with spiritual parenting, care and oversight of the adherence to a 'rule' of life. Although the 'rule' of life might not easily translate into our contemporary society the understanding and practice of spiritual parenting - unconditional love and care, setting an example, creating boundaries in which to exercise freedom, wise and gentle correction when necessary - would more easily be understood and embraced.

- At the heart of the Celtic Christian communities and their discipleship was a concept and practice which originated with the Desert Fathers - that of the 'Soul Friend' or 'anmchara' (Welsh 'periglour'). An older or more experienced person acted as teacher, confessor, mentor, spiritual director, and advisor. These relationships involved friendship at a deep level, with a concern for the spirituality of the other and guidance in spiritual matters.

The fundamental importance of these relationships is seen in the manner in which the Celtic Christian communities emerged - a recluse would go to a lonely, isolated place to live, word would spread, and people would gather to them to be discipled in common values and spiritual disciplines. It is possible to see here Jean Vanier's two key elements of community life being worked out - "The two essential elements of life in community are also a part of life in a family - personal relationship, and feeling you belong and are aiming to live towards a common goal and witness".[4]

CONNECT WITH FACETS OF COMMUNITY

M Scott Peck[5] has identified some of the many facets required for authentic community -

- Belonging - when you feel rooted, have identity and are able to become more of who you are.
- Openness - when you welcome the stranger.
- Vulnerability - when you can be seen, share who you are and risk being hurt.
- Caring - about the individual and their personal growth.
- Co-operation - when you work together from a shared experience of God's love and understanding that we are called to be together.
- A safe place to heal and grow - stay alone and we don't have to face our issues, community brings it all to the surface, but people listen and care and walk with us and help us to meet with Jesus.
- Forgiveness - when you walk in grace instead of judgement and understand the cry behind the action.
- Trust - grows out of each forgiveness. We learn we are accepted and trusted by others so we can trust ourselves.
- Be yourself - because it is safe, we can be who we are, and be realistic.
- Share your weakness - we are all broken, and we understand we are human.
- Use your gifts - where each one has something to give.
- Live a commitment to others.

As an exercise in reflecting look at these facets of authentic community and journal a response. Has this been your experience? How could it become your experience?

HISTORY - ST. JOHN CASSIAN

Second only to the Scriptures, the Celtic monastics were most influenced in their spiritual practice by the writings of St. John Cassian. After wandering seven years among the Desert Fathers of Egypt, Cassian became the most celebrated teacher of the monks of Gaul. Through him, the devotional lives and practices of the Desert Fathers influenced the rise of "soul friendship" in Celtic lands.

John Cassian's Conferences emphasised that the key to discernment and safety from falling came

160

from sharing one's heart honestly in community. "An evil thought sheds its danger when it is brought into the open... Its dangerous promptings hold sway in us as long as these are concealed in the heart." This heart to heart sharing took place with spiritual mentors, pure of heart and free from judgement who can listen to the secrets of others. He also taught "Soul friendship," characterised by deep affection and intimacy. Soul friends deeply respect one another's wisdom and values, yet are able to challenge each other when necessary. Their relationship centred on God can survive the separation of time, locale, and even death.   Brad Jersak

VULNERABILITY AND "SOFT EYES"

Community is built when we are "empty" rather than full of our self and our own opinions. It means we learn to deny ourselves and our need to know. Being empty means we learn to depend on the Holy Spirit more and more, we take down the walls we have put up to protect ourselves and we learn how to listen. We learn to see each other - brokenness, frailty and weakness - through soft eyes rather than the hard eyes of judgement, criticism and our reactions.

We can build a deeper sense of community by doing the small things, showing gentle concern in the every day. Those small gestures of caring, the habitual acts of kindness and self-forgetfulness, those sacrifices which say 'I love you' and 'I'm happy to be with you', allowing someone else to go in front of you, not trying to prove that you are right in a discussion and carrying each others burdens all display a fundamental respect and love for others and a generate a communal sense of stability, unity and wholeness. This is primarily about the 'other-centredness' that is so much a part of Paul's letters to the early church - "Do not do anything out of jealousy or vanity; but in humility count others better than yourselves. Let each of you look not only to selfish interests, but to those of others" (Phil 2:3).

CONNECT WITH THE DIFFERENCE

Celebrate the difference and see with soft eyes -
- Think about someone you do not get on with, ask yourself the following questions. Write the answers down:-
- What do I like about him/her?
- How is she/he like me?
- How is she/he different from me?
- Are there times when I react to this person because they remind me of things in myself that I don't like?
- Ask Jesus to show you their brokenness and vulnerability.
- Pray for that person - thank God for what you like in the other person and for how they are different to you, pray for their weaknesses and their vulnerabilities and bless them.

MINI BLOG - COMMUNITY

Living in community is probably the hardest thing I have ever done. For it to be real, mean something, count for something, it has to cut deep. And it does. It means digging deep for reserves of grace, commitment, honesty, vulnerability, working through reactions to find my fears beneath, face them and bring them to Jesus for Him to deal with. At times it feels like walking across broken glass with no skin on my feet - excruciating shocks of pain.

The joys are equally unsurpassed - the times spent laughing, being, listening, talking, connecting deeply, working, travelling, eating together, communing together build safety in the present and for the future.

Deb Chapman

HISTORY - COMMUNITY

There was a common pattern to how the Celtic Christian communities were established. A recluse seeking solitude, withdraws to a cave or cell in a mountain or forest and around him a number of disciples soon gathered forming first a community. Each member had his own cell, till gradually their communal life developed into a monastery - founded on the ascetic principles and the ideals of the Desert Fathers, with rhythms of prayer and work, living in community and with retreats into solitude. In Celtic Ireland there were no large cities so monasteries were modelled on the pattern of the chieftain's fort or the schools of bards and druids which were self-contained and self-supporting surrounded by their own farmlands.

Wherever a small community, a church or a monastery was established they were not separate from the surrounding community but very much a part of the everyday life of the area. In Wales, the tribe or group of families whose life and worship were centred on a particular church would become 'Dewi's people', 'Teilo's people', or 'Padarn's people' taking their name from either the founder of the church itself or of the founder of the community of which he was a part. Wider connections were sought by creating a network of Christian communities based on the love of God and love of neighbour, held together by a common faith.[6] Whatever the size or shape of the community it took its values from its founder and each of the saints had their own distinctives - for example - Cadog.

Cadog had an insatiable appetite for learning and desiring to pass on his knowledge he established a monastic school at Llancarfan near Illtud's monastery at Llanilltud Fawr. These two monastic centres acted as channel ports and benefited from the important Irish traffic that passed to and from the continent by way of south Wales. It is likely that it was Cadog's thirst for knowledge that took him to Ireland and resulted in the connection with Finnian of Clonnard who was the man responsible for the development of the Irish monastic schools. Finnian's most famous pupil was Columba, whose monastery at Iona in Scotland became "one of the most important centres of learning [and also mission] in north-western Europe". Father John Ryan identifies Cadog at Llancarfan as the original source for the impetus for the great Irish intellectual movement which had such a profound effect on Europe from the end of the sixth century.[7]

162

CONNECT WITH BEING EMPTY

Group Activity - Stones in the cup

This is an exercise in deepening community through "emptying ourselves". It is not about emptying your mind as in Eastern meditation, but rather about filling ourselves with Jesus.

- Need cup, stones in the cup.
- The stones represent our judgements, opinions, unmet expectations, disappointments with people, prejudices, offences, hurts and wounds that stop us listening to someone.
- Group stays in a circle and spends 3 minutes in silence asking Jesus to show them if there is anyone in the group they are holding judgements, hurts, opinions against.
- Leader settles the group, leads them through a prayer. "Lord Jesus would You show me by the Holy Spirit if there are any stones in my heart that You want me to give to You today. Amen".
- Leader asks them to hold a three minute silence whilst they listen to Holy Spirit and think about this.
- After 3 minutes, lead them through a prayer of saying sorry for having these stones in their heart and asking Jesus to help them, as they pray they can take the stones out of the cup. "Lord Jesus I am sorry that I have these stones in my heart towards... (ask them to name the people quietly) and I choose to forgive those who have hurt me and ask You to forgive me for making judgements about my friends in the group. Lord Jesus if there is anything You want me to see or hear or know I ask that you would reveal it to me now. Amen".
- Leader asks the group to wait in silence or another minute for them to listen to God.
- Leader asks for voluntary feedback -
- Did they understand what the stones were?
- How did they feel doing the exercise - explain there is no right answer - uncomfortable? scared? angry?...
- Did anyone become aware of stones in their heart and want to share what happened with them.
- Anyone want to share what God said/did.

Summary -

One of the key ways to build community is to practise being "empty" so that we can be filled with more of Jesus. The key to being empty is to quieten our own thoughts and ask God what He wants to say, which takes humility. We learn to listen to him and other people.

Deb Chapman

CREATIVITY - LIGHT

The monastic communities of the early Celtic church were holistic in expression and creativity was a marked value amongst them.

The monasteries became centres of learning and particularly in Ireland furnaces for the birthing of literature and art. They provided a haven for craftsmen fleeing from the Anglo Saxon invasion.New skills developed including millefiori glass - "a thousand flowers"- fused and worked into bundles of glass rods.

CELTIC CROSSES

The Celtic crosses which developed told a story in their artwork and painting. A cross within or breaking through a circle spoke of the glory of Jesus transforming every aspect of creation The symbol of the cross was understood whether or not people could read or write.

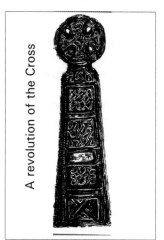

A revolution of the Cross

They were often carved with intricate, abstract designs which reflected the mysteries of God. They arrested people with majesty and marked meeting places of prayer and preaching.

These crosses were visual billboards, telling a story calling for a response. They were the home pages of a vibrant faith which embraced a rich creativity and would originally have been painted in rich colours, reds, blues and yellows, again proclaiming something of the victory of Jesus over pagan religions of fear and twilight.

The crosses and the carving of Christian symbols on pagan worship centres - circles and stones - were also a reminder to the spiritual realm of a change of allegiance. They were the spoils, along with the people, of power encounters - resonating with echoes of Elijah and Mount Carmel.

The Nevern Cross

BOOKS

The Book of Kells consisting of the four gospels of the New Testament was illustrated in incredible delicate lettering, bizarre creatures and rich colour. Originally it would have been bound in a gold cover and encrusted with jewels - too precious for every day use it would have been displayed on the altar for special occasions.

This was not the case with the pocket gospels, The Lichfield Gospels compiled in Llandeilo, The Book of Armagh and The Book of Durrow. The gospel message of the life of Jesus was spread through the scribes and artists who produced them and the monks who carried them in leather satchels.

The monks with their shaved heads and long pony tails took the look of outcasts and slaves as they walked the land for the love of Jesus. These books were the hi-tech equipment of their day they were THE cutting edge of innovation and communication. They were the forerunners - where and who are the forerunners today?

Creativity can be a marked value amongst us now. It finds a safe place in community and also connects us to wider community - a local new age commune had no problem understanding our expression of church as creative community. It is a privilege and a challenge to try and connect with such communities and people in a way that is both loving and wise. Loving those caught in a tangle of searching and journey and often deception and deep occultism; looking for places of understanding often in the midst of stark power encounters. Jesus is looking for those who will love enough, be humble enough and yield enough to His wisdom to be "eye-openers" in these communities of the hungry.

We long to raid the treasure chambers of Heaven for a creativity which will draw a culture to unfurl before the light. Isaac the Synon called people - "to enter the treasure chamber that is within you and then you will discover the treasure chamber of heaven. For they are as one and the same. If you succeed in entering one you will see both. The ladder to this kingdom is hidden inside you in your soul".[8] We can raid the treasure chambers of heaven for a creativity which will break open our culture.

Worship in paint and film, in any media, can connect culture with heaven's sight and values. It tastes of a kingdom breakout into a sphere which is often more prophetic than the church. It is a release of the seers in a touch and sight generation.

At a New Age Festival we went to there was a lot of story telling, much of it noisy with fear... It tasted of pagan fires lit down many generations to warm the darkness invoked. The words and music rose as small flames of truth, jewels with echoes of eternity but no great light.

We long for creativity luminous with hope, drawn from the meeting place of the heart.

> # The best attribute for a painter is the divine flame.
> Jack B Yeats

ENAMEL

Glass crushed to powder
placed on sheet copper,
worked and etched and moulded,
Fired till black and burnt and ruined,
or so it seems,
until the fire light dances orange
and glass flows richly molten, searing,.
Dangerous glory,
Heavens glass and sight
To copper of our humanity.
Burnt treasure forged in furnace fire
and dance.

CONNECT WITH CREATIVITY

Reflection point.

- Ask Him where He wants to meet you.
- Worship Him there.
- Ask Him how he expresses creativity through you.
- Ask Him to lead you on an adventure of creativity.
- Ask Him to show you how you can encourage creativity in the community you are part of.

SUE'S BLOG

A Welsh woman living in Surrey, Sue had been given a picture of "Wild Fire Revival" created by someone who carries a heart for Wales. It had meant a lot to her to receive this. She put the picture on to the wall of her house. Many people admired it.

In November 2004 when she moved to a new house the Lord spoke to her that there would be strong opposition to the Wild Fire breaking out and she needed to ensure that she, as a fire carrier, didn't allow herself to be contained. She was to take the picture to various places and continue to fan the flame of revival.

In October 2005 she went back to the place she had received the picture. That same evening (the last one of a conference) Sue took the Wild Fire picture along with the oil representing joy (strength) and healing from Europe and scented Oil from Shetland (obedience) - and placed them at the front of the meeting as an indication that whatever was fresh and rising from within Wales... she wanted, not for herself, but to carry to England and then into Europe.

Friends prayed for her and her husband and blessed them. All the oil from Europe and also from Shetland was poured over the picture. It was a powerful time. There were prophecies and declarations. Amongst it all the picture broke away from the nails and wood. The oil, was mopped up with sackcloth.

The Lord spoke to Sue that she shouldn't mend the picture when she got home but should carry it around with her wherever she went in England. It spoke to her about the fresh wave coming, being birthed out of humility, brokenness, and extravagant generosity.

So, this is what she did. She took it to hotels when she had lunch with friends, to prayer groups she was involved with, to Lincoln when she stayed with friends there. Each place she went she simply prayed that people and cities would be impacted.

Later, at a time of a significant meeting in Birmingham she felt she should leave it there in the heart of the nation, as the Wild Fire picture seemed to encapsulate so much of what was taking place. She didn't know what would happen to it. Maybe the person she gave it to would re-make it and hang it on the wall in the prayer room of her church, perhaps the Lord would commission her to do a prophetic act with it...she might bury it in the land...use it as a bridge or give it to another nation...who knows??! But for now something of the wildness of the Spirit and of the fresh fire that is within Wales has been deposited with her in the heart of the UK for Europe, Africa the nations and for such a time as this.

Sue Erasmus

MINI BLOG - IS IT OK?

"Is it ok to be creative, to express things in paint and words when suffering in the world is so extreme and overwhelming? I feel torn, for in many ways I feel I worship as much in paint as words and lifestyle. Is it simply indulgence? It feels like part of our DNA, - it must be Your DNA, the DNA of heaven because it seems irrepressible even in the midst of great pain. What do you think Father? I need to know".

Creation

He said: Welcome to the future, Son.
You will shape
You will form
You will create.
I am bringing you out
To a wide place.
No limits.
A nation.
Prepare for the future
That I have for you.
We are going to create together
Because I am a creator
And so are you.
We are going to create together.
Before you is an empty canvas.
I am going to teach you My ways
And principles of creation
By My Spirit. So…
Create.
I said:
I will.
And I did.

Steve Smith

UNENDING SONG - NEW SOUND

There is a felt need for 'Holy Space' where the presence of God and the angelic is so tangible that it can be touched and felt - somewhere to 'be in His face'. We need to live in His presence amongst community - salt, but there is also need for a place where He is tangible, a place of light, where he can be clearly felt and experienced.

Pete Grelg has described the 24-7 prayer rooms and 'boiler rooms' as 'a living room - a place where the Father waits for his children to come and climb into his loving arms, a place where we can experience peace so that we can make peace later'.[9]

24-7 Prayer rooms and many other places of prayer and worship across the world, in bizarre settings or religious buildings are seeing fresh expressions of prayer released in creativity. In the visual - artwork, graffiti, non-verbal prayer. Poetry, music, symbols , candles, oil and icons, painted feet, and rooms trashed with mud, stones and sand, water features not as refined symbol but as buckets of wet blessing. It's mad but it captures something of another facet of prayer. At least it's not as extreme as the Celtic monks, practice of standing in the waves all night and praying!

The Celtic monks also expressed their prayer and worship in more traditional forms. St. Illtyd's monastery in Llantwit Major was one of only three sites of continuous prayer and worship in the British Isles, Glastonbury and Old Sarem being the other two. This style of singing came from the Eastern churches via Gaul. The Breton life of Samson mentions a deacon who 'had sung the gospel and prayer'. Chanting of Psalms formed a central part of the worship at Dewi's monastery. During the lifetime of Cadog in Llancarfan there was a reference to the 'giving of thanks and rejoicing, prayers and spiritual hymns'.

Their use of the Psalms was prolific. The Psalms have something to say about our lives and the state of the world; the monks in their singing and praying of the Psalms were constantly bringing the world before God and God before the world. It was a constant washing of human frailties in a tough honesty and the cry of the individual as part of a louder, wider cry of worship or cry of pain. This washing of the feet of Jesus and this foot washing of the world continued day and night. At times I am sure they were conscious of the sound of heaven, the voice of angels as suddenly, at first imperceptibly, the singing became richer and stronger than was possible with human voices alone.

GO DEEPER WITH CONTINUOUS PRAYER AND WORSHIP

DAVID'S TABERNACLE

Continuous prayer and worship is not a new phenomenon. It dates back to the time of David who instituted 24 hour continuous prayer and worship before the ark of the covenant in the special tent (tabernacle) he built for it. It differed from the tabernacle of Moses in that there was no veil to separate the people from the glory of God. David understood that the Lord inhabits the praises of His people and so instead of the veil David put singers and musicians (4,000 musicians and 288 singers) to minister in shifts 24 hours a day.

The tent may have been positioned on the earth on a mountain in Jerusalem but in the Spirit they were connecting and agreeing with the continual worship and intercession that takes place around the throne of God in heaven. This alignment with heaven has an effect upon the earth, Mike Bickle notes, "This agreement is called praise. Praise is not an ego boost for God. Praise brings the created order into agreement with Him releasing His life on behalf of His creation".[10]

The ideal model of worship in Spirit and in truth is seen in Revelation 4 and 5 around the throne where the beauty of the Lord is displayed, this model holds the keys to sustaining and enjoying 24 hour continuous prayer and worship - Harp and Bowl - the harp speaks of God's music and worship songs, the bowl speaks of intercession, both flowing together.

In Acts 15:14 -18 the apostle James in dealing with a crisis of the basis on which the Gentiles are saved quotes Amos 9:11, God's promise to rebuild David's tabernacle which has fallen down and we can see David's insight that the heavenly order of intercessory worship is vital to the gospel impacting all the nations of the earth.

"God has chosen to restore the Tabernacle of David as one essential element in releasing fullness of revival in the nations".[11]

David's Tabernacle has kingly, priestly and prophetic dimensions -

- Priestly - focused on 24 hour continuous prayer and worship following the Davidic principles.

- Kingly - focused on the apostolic ministry with power, fulfilling the great commission - evangelism, community, equipping and governmental role - determining what is allowed and not allowed access.

- Prophetic - focused on the release of the prophetic ministry on the church Acts 2:17

Willie Soans (church leader Mumbai,India) has noted that every time a king of Israel instituted a Davidic order of worship in the Temple spiritual and military victories came soon afterwards:-

1.	David	1 Chron 15-16	1050BC
2.	Solomon	2 Chron 5-7	1010BC
3.	Jehosophat	2 Chron 20	896BC
4.	Joash	2 Chron 23-24	approx 835BC
5.	Hezekiah	2 Chron 29-30	726BC
6.	Josiah	2Chron 35	623BC
7.	Ezra	Ezra 3:10-13	536BC
8.	Nehemiah	Neh 12:28-47	446BC

Important scriptures to David's Tabernacle -

Seven main chapters - 1 Chron 13, 15, 16, 23, 25, and 2 Chron 29.

Others - Zech 4, Haggai 1-2, Isaiah 4, Psalms 132-4, 148-150, 2 Chron 5-7, 1 Cor 12-14, Heb 7-10, Rev 4-5.

Deb Chapman

Since the summer 2005 a few of us have been in the 'Upper Room', praying and singing the Psalms. I can well understand the love the Celtic monks had for this type of prayer and worship. The experience of music, singing and praying scripture, antiphonal singing[12] all flowing together has been at times beyond words. This is not a structured programme but a free fall in the Spirit, waiting on His presence to catch the wind and hear His heart afresh in scripture. An engagement with God, body, soul and spirit.

We have entered the reality of the throne room together, angels, angelic voices in the room, a wild surfing of the waves of His presence as the Holy Spirit directs and leads the sounds, voices and prayers. A sense of wielding corporate authority over real life situations, prophetically calling forth that which does not exist or just simply gazing upon the beauty of His face, lost in wonder at His incredible grace that He should come. I have been amazed at the relevance and power of the Psalms for everyday situations when you start to sing them, they take on new meaning and application, and it is possible to be strategic and aim at very clear targets before being caught again by a wave of worship.

We have entered the throne zone where as David knew, "In Your presence there is fullness of joy: at Your right hand there are pleasures evermore". (Ps 16:11). The Celtic monks had many disciplines to sustain themselves on their journeys and I am sure this was one of them - I love it, it's addictive!

Deb Chapman

HISTORY OF CONTINUOUS PRAYER AND WORSHIP

In his book "Bangor Light of the world", Ian Adamson traces the history of continuous prayer and worship up to the time of Comgall at Bangor, N Ireland.

David instituted continuous prayer and worship in the tabernacle and it was intermittently maintained in the temple in Jerusalem. Exile in Babylon was a major disruption but upon return from exile it was reinstated.

In the inter-Testamental period the temple worship continued uninterrupted apart from 3 years 168-165BC during which time it was desecrated in 168BC. In 165BC the Jews regained independence and restored purity of temple worship.

ESSENES

Many Jews had fled into the desert in 168BC and formed the Community of Righteousness from which the Essenes developed. From the time of the destruction of the temple in Jerusalem in AD70 the Essenes of Egypt were perhaps the only community on this earth practising continuous praise and worship.

COMMENT

This flight into the desert echoes the escape into the desert by the later Christians who removed themselves from the "Constantine church" and the desecration of what they held pure. Their life rhythm and focus was perhaps an influence on Anthony as there are marked similarities with the rhythm of solitude, silence, coming together weekly for communion, austere lifestyle of Anthony and his followers. There is no specific mention of corporate continual worship and intercession but Martin of Tours who was deeply influenced by Anthony brought this aspect in to the foundation of his first monastery at Marmoutiers.

PATRICK

Mabillon stated that Martin had early on adopted the Laus Perennis and that a young Patrick also visited Martin at Marmoutiers to take part in it as part of his preparation for his mission to Ireland. Parick's faith was so deep that it was said of him that, "each night he sang a hundred psalms to adore the king of angels." . Patrick had established and also founded Movilla in County Down where Columba was educated and Comgall helped Columba in his mission to Scotland.

BANGOR

Comgall studied under Finnian at Clonenagh and also founded Bangor (northern Ireland) in the Valley of Angels in 558AD. It was one of the most famous monasteries and missionary schools in Western Christendom. Along with Bangor on the Dee (Wales) and Iona (Scotland) formed a trio of great centres of Celtic Christianity in the British Isles.

"The strength of the community lay in its form of worship. The choral services were based on the antiphonal singing from Gaul, introduced into the west by Ambrose of Milan in the fourth century. Bangor became famous for this type of choral psalmody and it spread from there throughout Europe. The glory of Bangor was the celebration of a perfected and refined Laus Perennis... Because of the 3,000 students and monks in Bangor and its daughter churches, it was possible to have a continuous chorus of the Divine Praise sung by large choirs which were divided into groups, each of which took regular duty and sang with a refinement not possible when Martin was organising the raw recruits of Gaul".[13]

The continual prayer and worship the monks practised sustained them on their journey. Whether amongst their home community or wandering for the love of God, it is clear from the acounts of their lives that they considered the recital of psalms and prayers a major weapon to overcome the world, the flesh and the devil.

Could the focus on continuous prayer and worship be a factor in the evidence of the supernatural and presence of angels amongst those who practised it - David's Tabernacle, Temple at Jerusalem, Anthony, Martin, Patrick, Comgall at Bangor - all these point to the alignment and agreement of heaven and earth and the release of, "Thy Kingdom come Thy will be done on earth as it is in heaven". There is the release of the power and life of God through this type of spiritual warfare.

TIM'S BLOG

LEVITES JOURNEY AND THE NEW SONG

Four years ago I left a police career of 18 years and went self-employed as a video producer. This was a big step for our family bringing a mix of both exciting and stretching times. The first two years saw doors flying open and contracts coming thick and fast. Then suddenly between June and December 2004 we had no less than seven jobs fall through which led me into a time of depression (and painting and decorating!).

By summer 2005 and a hefty business overdraft, we decided to hold the business out as a 'fleece' for the next six months asking the Lord to either draw it to a close or cause a significant turn around.

In October, a number of strange incidents happened including my business website and e-mail being out of action for 3 weeks. My video editing computer, along with monitors and other equipment also suffered significant damage through a power surge. It was so in my face that I realised God was trying to get my attention.

THE VISION

In November 2005, He gave me a vision of a crucible full of molten silver. It was very clear but that was all, nothing else. In the middle of this turbulent time, He was drawing me into His presence, and showing me more of His beauty. This was birthing in me a 'lovesickness' to be with Him.

RETREAT

I decided to spend a short time away alone at a friend's farm and it was there where He unfolded more revelation about the silver crucible. Once away, I started to draw together a list of personal prophetic words and dreams He had given me from my childhood to the present. It gave me something of an overview, seeing the thread of His word to me through the years. Music and worship has been an integral part of my life and this theme has featured strongly in these words and dreams. As a young married couple, my wife and I received a word that we would have Levitical calling on our lives being involved in praise and worship, which would extend to our family. This has been borne out over the years with our consistent involvement in this area of church life.

THE DREAM OF A NEW SONG

In 1996, I had the most vivid dream I've ever experienced. I was in an army hut in the middle of the jungle. I was with a small unit of soldiers. It was hot and humid and the soldiers were undisciplined and lazing around. A sergeant major came in and immediately started to shout orders. The soldiers began to leave the hut, shrugging off the commands and I was left alone in the hut with the officer bearing down on me, in my face, shouting. It was a place of hard discipline.

Just then, he left and I began to hear the sound of drumming. Two soldiers entered the hut playing snare drums with pipes and cymbals attached to the drums. Then a line of pipers came in playing a strong Celtic melody. This melody unfolded as line after line of musicians entered the hut. I could see musicians and worshippers from many nations. An Indian girl was dressed in a sari playing an ebony flute. I was totally overwhelmed and was crying at the incredible symphony of this music. I remember saying to myself, "This is the new song, this is the new song". And I was acutely aware that it was God's composition, so much beyond my own gifting or capability. At that point I woke up and had tears in my eyes. The melody was still playing in my head and I went downstairs to play it on my guitar. I'm unable to write musical notation and had to keep playing the melody over and over in my head all day (in work!) until I could get together with my friend in the evening to notate it. I eventually managed to do this and wrote the instrumental 'Dream of a new song'. This song along with others birthed in me a desire to be part of many releasing the glorious sound of heaven - the new song.

PROPHETIC WORDS

The Levitical theme came up again in prophetic words I received in 1999 and 2001, particularly around the character of Asaph. His name means 'Gatherer' and he was one of the chief musicians along with Heman and Jeduthun appointed by King David to establish the twenty-four hour praise and worship at the tabernacle of David. He also was the author of some of the Psalms. Years after David's reign, 128 of Asaph's descendants returned from the Babylonian exile to participate in the restoration of the temple and its worship.

With the encouragement and vision of the leadership at our church in Llanelli, I started to look at serving and developing the worship and prayer room here. It's obvious to say that this is something that cannot be achieved overnight, but the desire and vision for this continues to grow in me.

SILVER IN THE SCRIPTURES

On the second day of the retreat I started to look at the significance of silver in scripture and He began to unfold more of the vision of the molten silver.

In Numbers 10:1, God told Moses to make two trumpets from 'hammered' (NIV) or 'one piece' (KJV) of silver, one for calling the people worship at the tabernacle and the other to sound in times of warfare. These were to be blown by Aaron and the Levites. These themes appear again in Revelation 8:6 and 11:15 with the seven angels and the seven trumpets.

THE INTERPRETATION OF THE VISION

I asked Him to show me what the molten silver crucible was about. I then saw Him pick it up and pour the silver into two trumpet- shaped moulds. He then showed me my wedding ring, which is white gold (silver coloured) and said, "You are married to me! You are married to me"! I then remembered that earlier this year I had to have the ring broken and enlarged to fit my finger. He said that he was increasing my capacity to hold the things He had for me in this following season. I then turned to Malachi 3:3, 'He [the Lord] will sit as a refiner and purifier of silver. He will purify the Levites and refine them like gold and silver that they may bring offerings of righteousness'.

In Deuteronomy 21:5 and 1 Chronicles 16:41 the root word 'chosen' of the Levites means 'highly polished, shining or reflecting'. The ephod or shoulder piece worn by the Levitical priest is rooted in the word 'image'. The female word 'ephuddah' refers to the plating of metal. I began to see the analogy of worship being reflected back to the King of Kings. At this point I felt Him lift the crucible of molten silver and begin to pour it into my mouth. It went down into my body and plated itself on my chest. It was a profound moment for me.

THE APPLICATION

What does this mean for me? Well, along with family and friends I'm still processing much of this and the outcome I believe will unfold over time. Like many others across the nations, I'm feeling a greater desire to see an establishing of a canopy of continuous prayer and worship but only something birthed in Him will have longevity, relevance and sustainability.

The teaching of, and imparting of musical gifting and worship to others is also a long standing passion of which I have dipped in and out over the years, however, it is significant that I have started guitar tuition this last year- more accident than design. I've also been delighted to see my two sons taking a group of enthusiastic, fiery and gifted musicians and shaping them in the arena of worship and musical skills.

For now, I believe my response is to align myself before Him and have the grace and courage to make another choice to trust Him for the future. Brennan Manning puts it beautifully and succinctly in his book, 'Ruthless Trust' -

"The way of trust is a movement into obscurity, into the undefined, into ambiguity, not into some pre-determined, clearly delineated plan for the future. The next step discloses itself only out of a discernment of God acting in the desert of the present moment. The reality of naked trust is the life of a pilgrim who leaves what is nailed down, obvious and secure and walks into the unknown without any rational explanation to justify the decision or guarantee the future. Why? Because God has signalled the movement and offered it His presence and His promise'.[14]
                                                                                    Tim O'Hare

UNENDING SONG

To stand before the Lord of all the earth
and see what He sees, breathe His breath,
and let it resonate spirit to spirit -
deep sounding to deep.

To then breathe out upon charred, broken
land and lives the very breath that brings
life and release upon the earth the
prayer and worship of heaven.

Breathe in the air of heaven
Breathe it out upon the earth

    Breathe in the air of heaven
    Breathe it out upon the earth

        Unending Song
        Unending Song

Deb Chapman

Communities full of His sound and light where anyone can discover what it means to be "in His face" - in His presence. Safe places to set out from on wild adventures.

MOVEMENT

MOVEMENT

Patrick pushed to the extremes his fifth century adventures in God. In his own words He had taken the Gospel "to those parts of the earth beyond which nobody lives".[1] Within what was known in his day he had gone to the ends of the earth in taking the gospel to Ireland.

He described himself "as the sinner Patrick. I am the most unsophisticated of people, the least of christians...I was about sixteen when I was taken into captivity in Ireland - at that time I was ignorant of the true God - along with many thousand others".[2] He was taken there as a slave, found faith in Jesus escaped from Ireland and was called back in a dream.

"I saw a vision of the night; a man named Victoricus - like one from Ireland - coming with innumerable letters. He gave me one of them and I began to read what was in it: The voice of the Irish. And just as I was reading the letter's opening, I thought I heard the voices of those who live around the wood of Foclut which is close to the Western Sea. It was as if they were shouting with one voice: 'O holy boy we beg you to come and walk among us'. And I was broken-hearted and could not read more. Then I woke up. Thank God, after many years the Lord granted them what they called out for".[3]

He had also embraced extremes of adventuring in the Holy Spirit, he saw his experiences, his dreams and visions as a part of the fulfilment of end-time prophecies. He claimed the end of the world was coming very shortly; "In the last days, God says, I will pour out my spirit on all people.Your sons and your daughters will prophesy, Your young men will see visions, Your old men will dream dreams". (Joel 2:28).

This 'least of Christians' dared to believe that his life could radically impact the course of history - he was looking forward to "the day of the Lord "and doing every thing he knew" to speed its coming.

"Walk among us" is a cry which can be heard in our day, now, in every nation. He is looking for the "broken-hearted", those who are willing to have their hearts wrecked by the cry of the poor, the lost and walk amongst them like Patrick did. But many of us risk being stranded in past ways of living - once safe places that have now become prisons.

"STRANDED?"

"Walk on the headland at Rhosilli, check the tides are ok to walk across the reef rock causeway to Worms Head. Collect crab shells along the way - crab shells in vibrant shades of lilac and blue, the vibrant shades fade as they dry out. It is time to let go - parable of these years. Have been here once before - the causeway hidden like the links in memory only revealed at certain times, rocky and hard to cross. Island memory, a place of different view point, isolated, disconnected; a place to move on from, not a place to live.

There is the danger of being stranded, powerless except in the choice to go with the rhythm of the tide and the window of time on the rocky beach. Halfway back I set the shells and flowers adrift in the crossover point between then and now... transition. Again this day the choice - embracing moment, embracing movement".

We are being drawn into adventures in God in the twenty-first Century. We can take ground that has never been taken before. If this book has simply been an interesting read - please burn it - for that was never its purpose! It rather gives voice to an emerging grassroots movement of those passionate for His presence and the poor. This walked out in different ways by adventurers of the everyday in the ordinary and the extraordinary. They carry the mantle of St. David whose last words were about doing the small things.

It is a call to adventure in God - to break into new dimensions in Him so that new dimensions of His glory and life might break out amongst the desperate and the hurting. Adventures lived out in all the colours of His multi-coloured grace. It is time to get moving!

Patrick did in his day, there is an urgency in ours. We are in danger of getting stranded if we will not let go, there is a tide to catch - we will be powerless without it. There is a choice to embrace now and embrace movement.

> Txt this ...
>
> "New days upon us.
> Wild wind is rising.
> Heavens breath
> released.
> Here we go
> my friend"!

"This time I am not coming for a 100,000 but for the nations, glory flowing like molten gold to the people and places of least resistance, teams flowing, running - the message - My presence and the poor. Nations transformed, for the transforming of the nations".

FOOTNOTES

Introduction
1. Tyneside Salvation Army Council of War, May 1879.
2. John O'Donoghue, Anam Chara: Spiritual Wisdom from the Celtic World.

Detox - Intoxicated Life - Overview
1. Thomas à Kempis, The Imitation of Christ.
2. Eugene Peterson, The Contemplative Pastor - Returning to the Art of Spiritual Direction.
3. Henri Nouwen, The Return of the Prodigal Son: A Story of Homecoming.
4. Tim Severin, The Brendan Voyage.

Desert Journey
1. Workman and Reader. Evolutioninary Psychology.
2. Wolfgang Simpson.Houses That Change the World
3. Thomas Merton, Seeds of Contemplation.
4. Richard Foster, Streams of Living Water - Celebrating the Great Traditions of the Christian Faith.
5. Patrick Thomas, A Candle in the Darkness, Celtic Spirutality from Wales.
6. John Chryssavgis, In the Heart of the Desert, The Spirituality of the Desert Fathers and Mothers.
7. Madame Guyon, Experience the Depths of Christ.
8. Brother Lawrence and Frank Laubach, Practising His Presence.
9. Saint Patrick, Ian MacDonald.
10. Patrick Thomas, A Candle in the Darkness, Celtic Spirutality from Wales.

Journey of the Heart
1. John Chryssavigis, In the Heart of the Desert, The Spirituality of the Desert Fathers and Mothers.
2. Richard Foster, Streams of Living Water - Celebrating the Great Traditions of the Christian Faith.
3. Brad Jersak, Can You Hear Me?
4. Madame Guyon, Experience the Depths of Christ
5. Raphael Brown, The Little Flowers of St. Francis.
6. Teresa of Avila, The Inner Castle.
7. Julian of Norwich, Revelation of Divine Love.

Walk the Land, Carry His Presence
1. Friesen, Wilder, Bierling, Koepcke and Poole, Living from the Heart Jesus Gave You.
2. ibid.
3. Raphael Brown, The Little Flowers of St. Francis.
4. David Pott, Fountain Gate Community.
5. 24/7 website.

Journey to the Margins
1. www.drug-statistics.com.
2. Clairbourne, Christianity Today, September 2005.
3. Jeffrey Sachs, foreword by Bono, The End of Poverty.Economic Possibilities for Our Time.
4. www.24-7prayer.
5. Saint Patrick, Ian MacDonald.
6. Geoff Ryan, Sowing Dragons, Essays in Neo Salvationism.
7. ibid.
8. Bede, A History of the English Church and People. Penguin 1988.
9. Arthur Marwick, The Home Front.
10. Ben Wicks, No Time to Wave Goodbye.
11. Elizabeth Elliott, Chance to Die: Amy Carmichael Her Life and Legacy.
12. Heidi and Rolland Baker, There is Always Enough.
13. Wesley Campbell and Stephen Court, Be A Hero - The Battle for Mercy and Social Justice.
14. The Condensed World Mission Course - Reader 2nd Edition, Living Spring International.
15. Growing God's Kingdom from the Harvest. www.the-next-wave.
16. Viv Grieg.
17. Welsh Index of Multiple Deprivation 2005.
18. Jim Goll, The Lost Art of Intercession.
19. These facts are recorded by investigative journalist John Pilger in his book, The New Rulers of the World.

Wild Wandering
1. Richard Foster, Streams of Living Water - Celebrating the Great Traditions of the Christian Faith
2. Martin Robinson, Rediscovering the Celts - The True Witness from Western Shores.

3. ibid.
4. Anglo Saxon Chronicle, Parker Text.
5. Roger and Sue Mitchell, Target Europe.
6. Martin Scott, Impacting The City.
7. Michael Mitton, Restoring the Woven Cord.
8. Tim Severin, The Brendan Voyage.
9. Richard MacCullagh, The Irish Curragh Folk - Life on the Western Seaboard from Galacia to Greenland.
10. Geoff Ryan, Sowing Dragons, Essays in Neo Salvationism
11. Pete Grieg, The Vision.
12. Boiler Rooms, 24/7 prayer.
13. Ray Simpson, Exploring Celtic Spirituality.
14. Ian Bradley, The Celtic Way.
15. Wisdom of the Sadhu, Teachings of Sundar Singh, complied an edited by Kim Comer.
16. Chesterton, St. Francis of Assisi.
17. The Message, 1 Cor 4:9-13 and 2 Cor 4:8-12.

Keys of Heaven's Sight - Kingdom Breakout.

1. Roger and Sue Mitchell, Target Europe.
2. Sian Victory, The Celtic Church in Wales.
3. {atrick Thomas, A Candle in the Darkness, Celtic Spirutality from Wales.
4. John J. O'Meara, The Voyage of St. Brendan: Journey to the Promised Land.
5. Thomas Taylor B.D., The Life of Samsom of Dol.
6. ibid.

Sound and Light Community

1. Community of Friends in Renewal, Occasional Papers, a New Monasticism.
2. ibid.
3. Gem analogy, M.Scott-Peck.A Different Drum.
4. Jean Vanier, L'Arche Community, Switzerland.
5. M. Scott-Peck, A Different Drum.
6. Patrick Thomas, A Candle in the Darkness, Celtic Spirutality from Wales.
7. ibid.
8. Jim Goll, Consecrated Prayer Workbook.
9. Pete Grieg and Dave Roberts, Red Moon Rising.
10. Mike Bickle, Harp and Bowl Spiritual Warfare Syllabus.
11. ibid.
12. ibid,

13. Ian Adamson, Bangor Light of the World.
14. Brennan Manning, Ruthless Trust.

Movement
1. Thomas O'Loughlin, Saint Patrick The Man and His Works.
2. ibid.
3. ibid.

RESOURCES TO GO DEEPER

eXplore: based from Antioch, Llanelli, South Wales, involves experimentation and risk taking - the release of a radical mission movement amongst the poor.

To find out more about eXplore, please contact:

eXplore,
Antioch Church,
Antioch Centre,
Copperworks Road,
Llanelli,
SA15 2NE

Telephone: 01554 741674
e-mail: admin@explore123.wanadoo.co.uk
website: www.explore123.co.uk

24-7 prayer: Global communty of Christ-centred, mission-minded prayer.
Website: www.24-7prayer.com

World Horizons is a global mission movement which began in Llanelli, South Wales in the 1970's. Focusing on the unreached peoples of the world and emphasizing the importance of hearing God's voice for the nations it now has over 400 voluntary workers in 40 nations.

For more information on World Horizons, or its programme of mission trips, visit www.worldhorizons.co.uk or write to: World Horizons, Centre for the Nations, North Dock,

Llanelli, Carms, SA15 2LF.

Kairos (formerly Co:mission): A dynamic course designed to educate and mobilse Christians and churches into strategic 21st century, global mission. It encourages and challenges people to journey in their understanding of "being on mission with God" and what it means to live as "world Christians".

Contact: linda@kairoscourse.org.uk

Shedhead Productions: Part of the emerging creative community in Antioch, Llanelli.

Telephone: 01554 758080 or 749907
e-mail: shedheadproducts@aol.com
website: www.shedheadproductions.org

Booklets:
More in depth reading on some of the themes developed in this book are available in booklets -

Desert Training - Zoe Britnell.
Spiritual disciplines, rhythm of life, times of reflection and times of action.

Wild Adventuring - Zoe Britnell.
Practical steps to the mobilisation of wild wandering fire carriers.

Redeeming the Land - Pippa Gardner.
How prayer and intercession can contribute to the transformation of our communities and nation.

Remarriage of Church and Mission - Mark and Karen Lowe.

A Life Worth Living - Mark Lowe
A practical look at the restoration of faith in the everyday and its potential to transform communities.

Burnout? - Mark Lowe

Women in Leadership by Mark Lowe.
Have we made this issue too complicated? mark takes a straight look at the issues from scripture and from life.

Journey - Karen Lowe and Deborah Chapman.
Creative reflections, words, images, poetry and meditations to draw you deeper.

To order any of these booklets please contact Shedhead Productions and to view enamels, sculptures, pictures, jewelry please visit the website.

REFLECTIONS

The Spacious Place
Eden Jersak

He brought me out into a spacious place;
He rescued me because he delighted in me.
2 Samuel 22:20 (NIV)

The picture I see when imagining the spacious place is a beautiful mountain meadow. It stretches as far as the eye can see with beautiful vistas of spacious places beyond the one I find myself in. Mountain peaks and valley depths both visible from this vantage remain at a distance. The spacious place is neither lofty height nor dreary depth. It is a wide-open field, a safe place (2 Sam. 22:20), a place of comfort, a place without restriction (Job 36:16).

In this safe place, there is a table prepared for me. God has wooed me from the jaws of distress and danger and drawn me to the comfort of a table laden with choice food and blessings in that spacious place. His motivation in rescuing me is not some dysfunctional need to fix or enable, but rather, just the delight that He has for me. So when I find myself in the jaws of distress and danger, it's not my goodness or wisdom that somehow merits my being rescued. It is simply His delight in me at my most vulnerable, undone, end of my rope, messy and ugly moments. It may be easy to delight in me when I'm on my best behaviour, but when I'm in the jaws of distress and danger, I've probably done something stupid to find myself there! And still He provides a place, spacious and safe, free of restrictions and full of good things, just for me, because He delights in this woman in all her humanity.

He woos me to this spacious place. He doesn't demand my presence or take advantage of my precarious situation. He woos me. He calls me away from the jaws of danger and distress and invites me to a table filled with choice food and blessings. But I have a choice, and as obvious as it may seem, I have often turned my back on His invitation and chosen to stand dangerously close to the precipice. But His delight in me continues to compel Him to woo me to the safe place. And when I finally turn towards His warm and persuasive voice and take those first steps away from peril, I have already begun to enter the spacious place. I imagine Him taking both my hands in His... He walks backwards, holding my gaze and drawing me to a most wondrous sight: the spacious place.

I wondered if this place God has prepared for me is really Himself. It is broad, free, and a place where I am loved. I imagine that being in God's presence would be very much like that. God Himself is a table laden with choice food, and table burdened with blessings waiting for me.

I see Him, not at the end of the table, but right in the middle, with room on either side for me to come close. Gone are the dangerous jaws of distress. Instead, I sit beside my Rescuer as close as I can possible get. His compassion and mercy for my folly and His delight in my response to His invitation is evidenced by the grin on His face. I am about to partake of all that He has prepared – choice foods and bountiful blessings provided for me. He waits for me to enjoy them. I battle my unworthiness in being invited to such a lavish display of love and yet He continues to woo me to the feast of blessing.

I survey the blessings before me and wonder where to begin. What I see is a banquet of good things. There is favour in a large glass bowl. There is freedom on a platter. There is healing in a pitcher that doesn't seem to empty when being poured. Piled like fruit in a bowl are blessings of mercy and grace, joy and peace. Blessings of acceptance send off a fragrant aroma. Baskets of kindness and goodness flow over onto the table. And still more is arriving! The table is laden with blessings for me.

I look up from this overflowing banquet of blessings and survey the spacious place that surrounds me. I don't see fences or barriers of any kind. I only see freedom as far as the horizon, and then I see grace. This place that has been provided away from danger and distress is the very heart of God. He woos me to His heart, His table, and asks me to taste the blessings that He's prepared... because He delights in me... the one He has rescued from the jaws of danger.

Reflection on Spiritual Direction
Lorie Martin

Spiritual Direction is not spiritually directing a heart; it is spiritually looking directly with them into their heart. It is a time of co-discerning the movement(s) of God within them to discover what He is making known there. In listening together, Jesus Himself guides to places of revelation, understanding, and peace. One leaves after a relaxed, intentional time of spiritual direction encouraged and focused in the Lord's presence. – Lorie Martin, with deep thanks to her S.D., Karin Dart.